IRRESISTIBLE WATERS

Irresistible Waters

Fly Fishing in British Columbia Throughout the Year

Arthur James Lingren

FOREWORD BY STEVE RAYMOND

RAINCOAST BOOKS
Vancouver

First published in 1998 by

Raincoast Books
8680 Cambie Street,
Vancouver, B.C.,
V6P 6M9
(604) 323-7100

1   2   3   4   5   6   7   8   9   10

98   99   00   01   02   03

Maps courtesy of Environment B.C.
Cover photograph: Fishing guide Jill Hull casts for steelhead
in the Kispiox River, British Columbia. (Myron Kozak)
Myron Kozak photographs courtesy of the Driftwood Foundation,
RR #2, S-57, C-19, Smithers, B.C. V0J 2No.

CANADIAN CATALOGUING IN PUBLICATION DATA

Lingren, Arthur James.
Irresistible waters

Includes bibliographical references.
ISBN 1-555192-148-0

1. Fly fishing – British Columbia. I. Title.
SH572.B8L56 1998   799.1'24'09711   C97-910978-7

*Raincoast Books gratefully acknowledges the support of the Government of Canada
through the Book Publishing Industry Development Program, the Canada Council,
the Department of Canadian Heritage and the British Columbia Arts Council.*

PRINTED AND BOUND IN CANADA

To Beverley, my wife of over three decades,
for being patient and understanding about my other passion.

Contents

Foreword

"IRRESISTIBLE" IS A STRONG, unequivocal word and one does not use it lightly in the title of a book. But if you're an angler contemplating the wonderfully rich and varied waters of British Columbia, then no other word could possibly apply—for Canada's westernmost province is blessed with a long saltwater coastline, countless lakes and thousands of rivers, and nearly all are inhabited by some of the most sought-after gamefish in the world. Art Lingren has had the great good fortune to spend his life amid this wealth of water, and in the course of many years of fly fishing experience he has become intimately acquainted with British Columbia's gamefish. He admits he is most fond of steelhead—an understandable prejudice if you've ever caught one of these marvelous seagoing trout on a fly—but this feeling has never kept him from fishing for other species: the rainbow trout of B.C.'s interior lakes, the cutthroat trout of its coastal estuaries or the Pacific salmon that return seasonally to many of its rivers. Indeed, it may fairly be said that if it swims in B.C. waters and will take a fly, then Art has either caught it or it's on his list to do so.

Now, in this book, he shares some of his knowledge of the province, its waters and its fish. He has written the book for anglers new to the province, or new to fly fishing, or perhaps new to both—those who may be just a little overwhelmed by B.C.'s cornucopia of angling opportunities and uncertain exactly how or where to begin. Art offers sage advice, starting with an explanation of the physical geography of British Columbia and a list of some of its most important fly-fishing waters.

Ever mindful of the value and importance of tradition in British Columbia's angling culture, Art also offers a brief excursion through the province's colorful fly fishing history, then introduces B.C.'s splendid roster of gamefish—steelhead, rainbow, cutthroat and brown trout, five species of Pacific salmon, four species of char, kokanee, whitefish, Arctic grayling, pike and bass. He describes the tackle, flies and techniques needed to catch these fish in rivers, lakes or salt water, then details the seasonal fly fishing opportunities in each of the province's angling regions. Anecdotes from his own angling experience help sharpen the reader's appetite to try some of these waters.

But that's not all. In the back of the book you will find appendices filled with just the kind of practical information anglers need—licensing requirements, sources for maps and information about guides, resorts and fishing camps, a list of books and periodicals about British Columbia fly fishing, and more.

What a gift to anglers! Through the pages of this book, Art Lingren will get you started on the wonderful experience of fly fishing in British Columbia's irresistible waters. The rest is up to you.

Steve Raymond

Acknowledgements

WITH A FULL-TIME career and family responsibilities, putting a book of this nature together during weekends in the short four-month time allotted by my publisher certainly posed its challenges. I want to thank all those whom I contacted in my panic to fill my information gaps; I appreciate their response. To those of you who found me somewhat testy in my requests for information, I apologize.

A special thanks to Peter Caverhill for checking and providing comments on the game fish section and other information; to Van Egan for sharing his information, and for the use of his photograph; to Ron Schiefke for reviewing and commenting on the text; to Kelly Davison for sharing some of his Fraser River knowledge; to Brian Smith for his information on Region 7; to John Pehovich for information on Region 1; to Rob Brown for information on Region 6. And to all those other angling friends with whom I have wandered this province over many years, each of you added to my experiences and helped make this book possible.

Thanks to staff in provincial departments such those in Fisheries Branch, Forestry, Tourism and Parks for providing information. A special thanks to Minister Cathy McGregor and the Fisheries Branch for permitting the use of the eight regional and provincial overview maps and to those staff with whom I spoke individually or who responded by letter providing much needed information and filling voids.

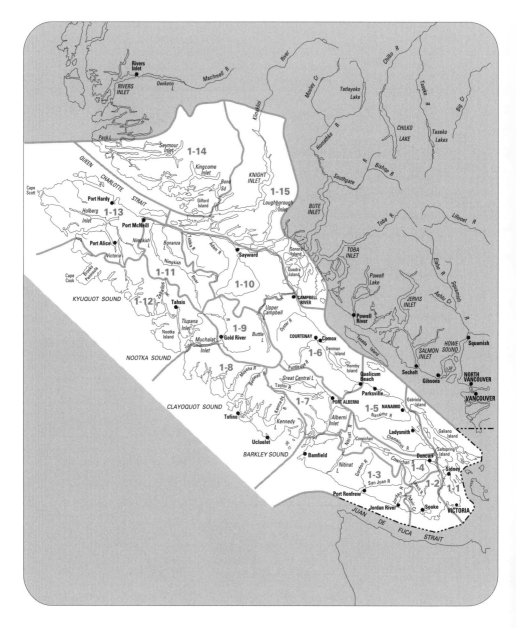

Region 1: Vancouver Island

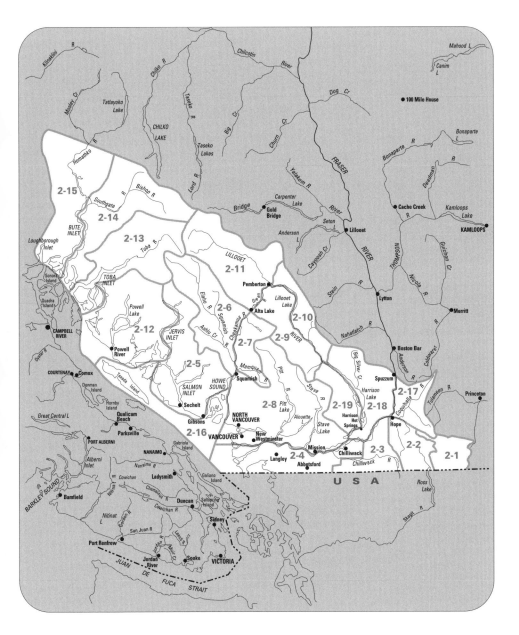

Region 2: Lower Mainland

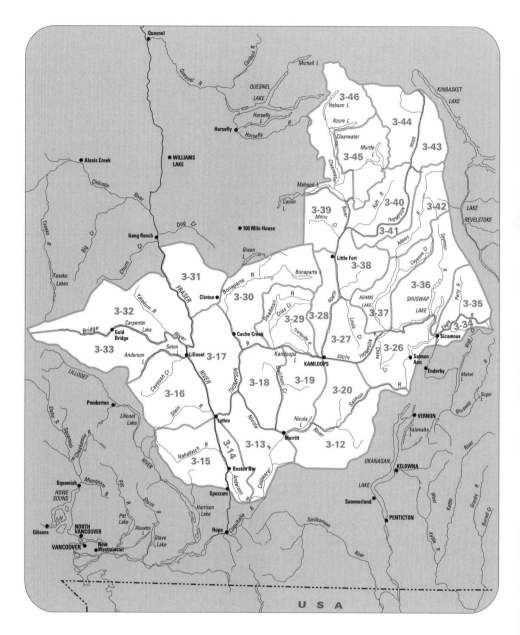

Region 3: Thompson–Nicola

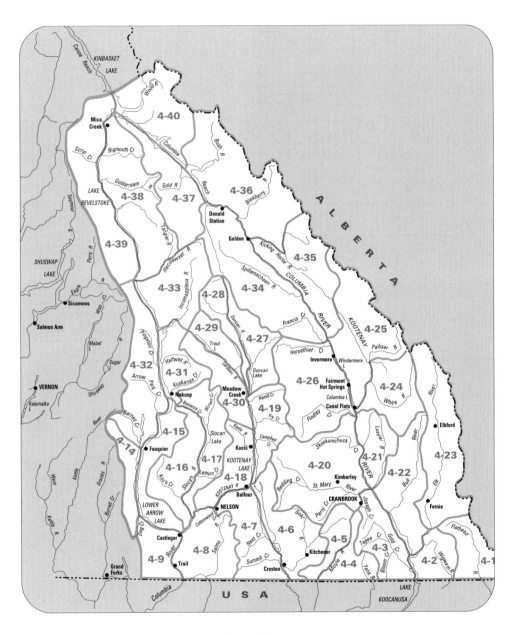

Region 4: Kootenay

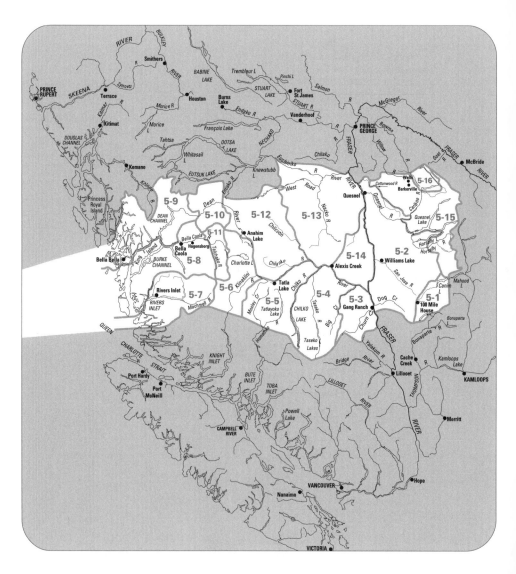

Region 5: Cariboo

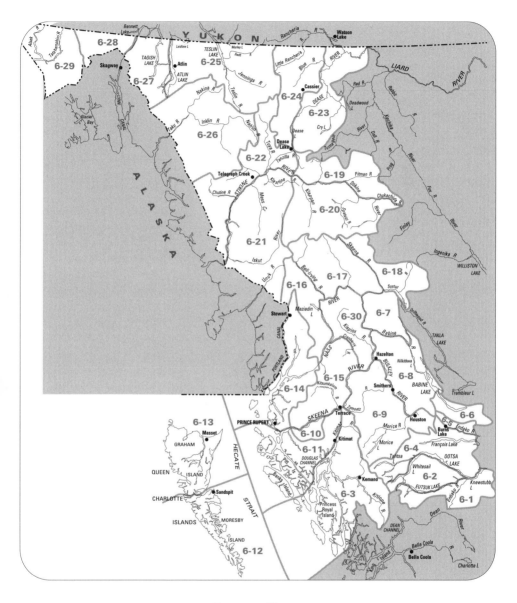

Region 6: Skeena

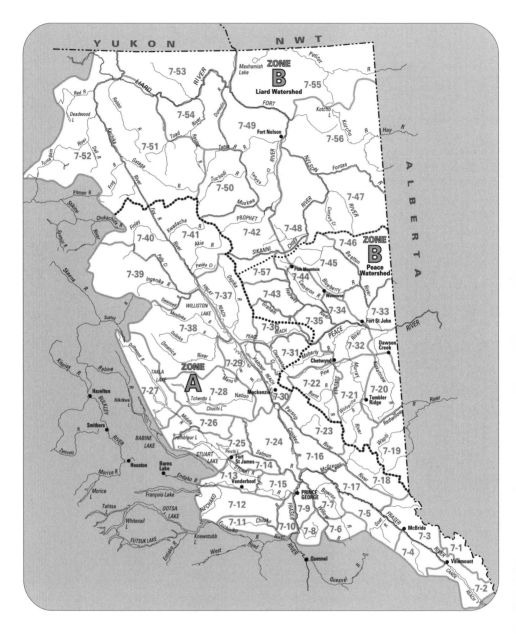

Region 7: Omineca–Peace

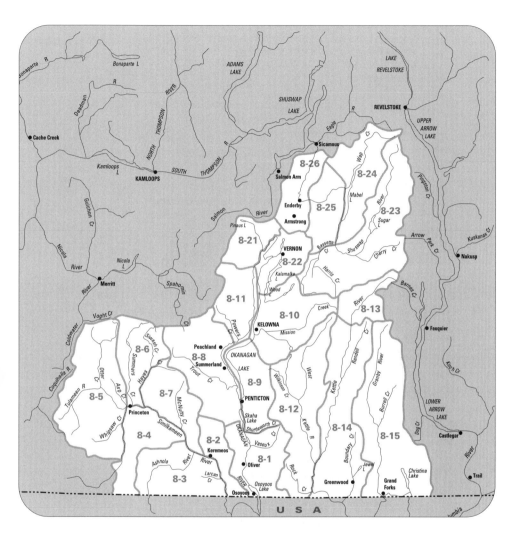

Region 8: Okanagan

CHAPTER ONE
Fly Fishing in British Columbia

I am a steelheader, have been one for over 30 years, and in the spring my pursuit of that fish takes me to Lower Mainland and Vancouver Island rivers. Because of poor steelhead returns during the winter and spring of 1997, fish to the fly were few and far between that year. In fact in nine days on the river from February through April I managed only one for-sure steelhead hook-up. But often when steelheading is slow other fish are there to fill the gap and new, sometimes unexpected experiences happen. They happen often enough to me that they cause me to reflect on my good fortune in living in British Columbia.

In the spring of 1997, on the Squamish River I took many Dolly Varden, topped by a 24½-incher [62 cm], my largest fly-caught dolly ever from that river system. On that same day I landed a 16½-inch [42 cm] cutthroat. The last cutthroat, and a small one at that, that I remember catching in the Squamish system, I took on the first year I fished the river, about 1965. On my excursions to Vancouver Island in the spring of 1997 I managed to hook and lose the only steelhead I connected with, but I will remember the large browns I caught as I wandered the trails and fished the Cowichan River.

Cutthroat and brown trout, Dolly Varden and steelhead—some of my favourite game fishes—all in one season, all within a short drive of my suburban home. Although not an exhaustive list, this is a good sampling of the variety of fishes and sport that Canada's most western province offers the adventurous fly fisher.

About the Province

British Columbia faces the Pacific Ocean on the west and shares borders with Alberta on the east and the Yukon and Northwest Territories in the north, besides being neighbour to four of the United States: Washington, Idaho, Montana and Alaska. It is a big province, with an area greater than Washington, Oregon and California combined. The Pacific Ocean exerts considerable influence on the coastal climate. However, because of its location in the northern hemisphere, the province's size and its mostly mountainous geography, the province's climate varies considerably from north to south and east to west.

It is mostly a mountainous province. The Rocky Mountains run from its border with the United States to the northern border with the Northwest Territories. Other ranges—such as the Columbia, Monashee, Cariboo, Selkirk, Purcell, Cassiar, Omineca and Skeena—run parallel to the coast. In all, three-quarters of the province's land mass is over 3,000 ft (900 m) above sea level. Only the Peace River region in the northeast corner of the province is considered flatland. This region became part of the province through the stroke of a mapmaker's pen. So little was known about the north that in 1861 when the boundary between Alberta and British Columbia was established, the cartographers followed the Rocky Mountain Divide until it intersected the 120th Meridian. They then drew the border straight north along that line to the Northwest Territories boundary.

Runoff from snow-topped peaks descends down the rifts, forming rivulets. Rivulets combine to make streams. Streams multiply on their journey through the valleys, becoming rivers. Along the way, depressions in the land fill and become lakes. All these together make British Columbia a fly fisher's paradise. However, there are other factors—climate, varying geography and soil conditions, small and concentrated population with vast unpopulated or sparsely populated areas that are difficult of access—that in one way or another individually or collectively influence the quality of fly fishing experiences. To accommodate fishing visitors, scattered throughout the province are fishing resorts which range from rustic cabins to luxurious lodges, and private, provincial and Forest Service campsites to match any fly fisher's budget.

About 12 percent of British Columbia's land mass is put aside for preservation, and much has park status, with many parks having campsites on lakes and rivers that have good fly fishing. Campsites such as Lac Le Jeune and Paul Lake near Kamloops, Juniper Beach near Ashcroft, Big Bar near Clinton, 10-Mile near Quesnel, Stoltz near Duncan and Elk Falls near Campbell River and Misty Meadows at Tlell come to mind that are all close by fly fishing waters. However, there are many more, and a good way of sampling an area is to plan a vacation using private, provincial or Forest Service campsites as bases and venturing out to nearby lakes and rivers.

Forestry practices have experienced widespread criticism in the past couple of decades, some well deserved. However, the system of logging roads has done more to provide access to public lands and waters than any other activity. Some say that with the network of logging roads access is made too easy. The pros and cons of resource extraction and access aside, the Forest Service in partnership with timber permit holders over the past 25 years has built a province-wide system of Forest Service recreation sites. Usually these sites are small, with a limited number of camping spots, a few picnic tables and an outhouse. Many are located on lakes or rivers. Some that come to mind are Moresby Camp near Sandspit, Hirsch Creek near Kitimat, Bimac near Houston, Hyas Lake near Pinantan, Tunkwa Lake near Logan Lake, Woss Lake near Woss. With 1,400 recreation sites spread throughout the province the list could go on and on. Unlike the provincial campsites, which have a day fee, there is no fee for using Forest Service campsites.

Beyond the developed campsites, much of British Columbia is wilderness crown land, and anglers often find clearings along rivers and lakes in which to set up camp. There are no restrictions about camping on publicly owned land, providing you use common sense and do not camp in places that hamper permit holders' business activities. However, whatever you take in on a camping trip, be prepared to take it out, especially non-burnable garbage. There is nothing more annoying than venturing into the wilds in search of solitude on a lake or river and finding some slob's garbage everywhere. Amenities such as those provided by Parks and Forest Service recreation sites permit more use of our public lands and waters. We should respect and value that right. Many people living in other countries in the world pay high fees, as much as $1,000 or more a day to fish some European Atlantic salmon waters, to enjoy what we take for granted.

If you examined a map of British Columbia you would notice that the 7,000-km (4,200-mi) long mainland coast has no road along it. Access to most coastal communities is by boat or plane. The main access route to the Cariboo, Chilcotin, Omineca and Peace communities and the coast is Highway 97, which leaves Highway 1 at Cache Creek. North of Cache Creek along Highway 97, Highway 20 branches west at Williams Lake and meanders through the Chilcotin Plateau and Tweedsmuir Park, then joins the coast at Bella Coola. Bella Coola is the Indian village where, in 1793, Alexander Mackenzie first saw the Pacific Ocean after his epic journey across Canada. Further north along Highway 97, Highway 16 branches northwest at Prince George, heading through the western part of the Fraser River watershed into the Skeena watershed, joining the coast at Prince Rupert. From Prince Rupert you can take a ferry across Hecate Strait to the Queen Charlotte Islands. However, there are many remote waters along the mainland coast and coastal islands that are worth exploring, given the time and money.

It is not uncommon for a Vancouver fly fisher to travel 150–250 km (90–150 mi) or more for a day's fishing. I do that when I go to the Skagit for a day. To go to the Interior lakes and rivers is a journey of 300 km (200 mi) or more, and distances such as those are common to fishers venturing out for a weekend. Others go farther afield on long weekends and holidays. There are main highways that traverse north, south, east and west, and there are many destinations in close proximity or along the main highways. The Lower Fraser, Harrison,

Coquihalla and Thompson rivers are examples that come readily to mind. Often fishing locations are off the beaten track, and the roads will vary from what is classed as secondary to nothing more than ruts in the dirt.

The further you travel on the secondary and backroads, the further you may be from help if you have mechanical failure or get stuck. Some backroads require four-wheel-drive, but winches should be also part of standard equipment, as should a first-aid kit. Ensure your spare tire is serviceable and tire changing equipment is in your vehicle when heading out onto the backroads. Some backroad travelers take along two spares depending on distance traveled, the remoteness and the roughness of the backroads. Many backroads are only one lane wide, and recreational vehicle drivers should make doubly sure where they are going before they venture onto those roads where turn-around may be difficult or impossible. I have a 20-year-old camper on the back of my pickup truck that has numerous skin patches caused by branches poking through the aluminum during my travels on tree-canopied backroads. Furthermore, I have ripped off five camper jacks by hitting stumps located on too narrow a road or when travelling along stump-lined, narrow roads in darkness.

Road conditions will vary with the weather, and fly fishers travelling on these backroads need to know that dirt roads can turn to gumbo and become quite slippery after a good rain or snowfall. Before venturing into the wilds, you need to know, as best as can be determined, accurate directions how to get to your desired destination, as well as current road conditions. Up-to-date maps are a must. However, because British Columbia's main economies are resource-extraction-based, forestry and mining companies are adding to the network of roads all the time and any tourist map you have is probably months if not a year or two out of date. All Forest Regions produce maps of their area, which are updated every second year. It is worthwhile contacting the local Forest Service office to pick up their latest map showing roads and recreation sites. Furthermore, if you know anyone who has been to the lake or stream you plan to visit, ask them about access, or ask local fishing shops if they know what access is like to certain waters. If you are staying at a resort, the owners will often provide local knowledge of nearby fishing waters and access. By doing some advance legwork, you may save yourself grief and avoid lengthy, time-wasting diversions.

Unlike the cities we escape from, which are well signed, when you get out into isolated areas road signs are few and turnoff signs to lakes are, more often than not, non-existent. It is by knowing that such and such a turnoff to a certain water is so far past a certain road junction that gets you to your destination. However, if you are heading to a resort and access is by backroad, resort owners want you to find their place, so they will post signs blazing the trail. Even then it is not hard to get waylaid, and unless you know the route, it is wise to try to find off-main road spots during daylight hours.

I remember the first time I went to Hihium Lake. Hihium has two public access roads: one that comes off Highway 97 along the Loon Lake Road that goes around the eastern end of Loon on a good Forest Service road to the lake's Forest Service campsite and to the resorts. The other access is off Highway 1 up the Deadman Creek/Vidette Lake road then onto a steep pipeline maintenance road. One of my co-workers wrote down directions for the Deadman Creek route, which he transcribed from his father. The directions seemed straightforward, so I did not take along my fishing directory, which gave turnoff distances and showed other roads. My co-worker's distances were wrong and I ended up taking a wrong turn and eventually found myself back at Highway 1. Part way along the turnoff, I suspected as much because the road I ended up on was recently constructed and not of the vintage I expected. Back I went to the Deadman Creek Road. I reasoned that I was going to a resort and that they would have their turnoff marked. I continued up the valley until I found a small white sign not much bigger that a foot square propped up with a rock beside the turnoff to a steep road directing me to Hihium Fishing Resort. I had left work at 2 p.m., thinking I might get a couple of hours fishing that evening. I ended up driving in the night through unfamiliar country, on poorly marked roads and arrived at 10 p.m., just in time to hit the sack. All said and done we woke the next morning to be greeted by a late spring snowstorm. Although my journey was long and drawn out the evening before, I realized then that it could have been worse if I had had to travel that steep road later that night. We should always be thankful for small mercies and I was thankful for mine.

Similarly, if you travel by boat in pursuit of elusive quarry, you ought to take sensible precautions. It doesn't matter where you go on open water, on the sea or on lakes throughout the province, you need to plan ahead and know how you will get back if you get caught in a storm. Wind, waves and small boats are a bad combination and can kill. Boat safely.

There are fishing directories with specific information on locations for many waters and often the type or condition of road will be noted. (Those references are listed in the Appendices.)

When most of Canada's other provinces and territories are in the deep freeze, there are places in British Columbia, even through the dead of winter, where fly fishers can cast their lines into flowing rivers and catch silver-bodied cutthroats, steelhead and other fish. In putting this book together, I have segregated the information into Fisheries Branch Management Regions through the seasons. Much of my information provides general guidance to fly fishers, but all must realize that it would take thousands of pages and many lifetimes of travel to create the definitive work on British Columbia fly fishing. Whole books can be written on regions or specific waters. For example, I have written books on two of my favourite rivers, the Thompson and the Dean, and they are devoted to the steelhead fishing with only cursory mention of the trout, salmon and other fishes available from those waters. However, we have to start somewhere.

The *British Columbia Freshwater Fishing Regulations Synopsis* breaks the regions down into smaller management units for locating more closely certain waters. The synopsis plus other supplementary references to more specific types of fly fishing or locations are a must for visiting fly fishers. (A list of those available is included in the Appendices.)

There are many classified waters in the province which, because of their quality fishing, demand special attention. Anglers are lured to these quality waters because of their unique fisheries. British Columbians must purchase a separate classified waters license, good for all classified rivers, while visitors from outside the province, to enjoy the same access to these waters, must pay a daily-use fee.

The Fishing Regions

REGION 1: VANCOUVER ISLAND

This region includes Vancouver Island proper, adjacent islands and a section of the mainland southeast of Sayward, north to about the northern tip of the Island and northeast to the end of Knight Inlet.

I have fished Vancouver Island waters for more than 30 years and have many fond memories from catching steelhead, coho salmon, cutthroat, browns and rainbows from many waters in this region. Rivers like the Cowichan, Campbell, Stamp and Nimpkish are steeped with angling lore. The Cowichan River has testimonials to its quality fishing dating back to the 1880s. Of course, the Campbell River is Mecca to many North American fly fishers because it is the place that North America's most revered fly fishing writer, Roderick Haig-Brown, lived and fished for so many years. Through the 1930s to the 1960s Haig-Brown provided ample documentation in *The Western Angler* (1939), *A River Never Sleeps* (1946), *Fisherman's Spring* (1951), *Fisherman's Summer* (1954) and *Fisherman's Fall* (1964) of Region 1's fly fishing.

The Vancouver Island region, even with the huge population increases of the 1980s and 1990s, provides fly fishing opportunities for rainbow, brown and cutthroat trout, steelhead, salmon and bass throughout the year. Anglers will find fly fishing experiences that range from those associated with heavily fished streams such as the Cowichan, Stamp and Campbell; to those expected on more remote rivers such as the Marble and Mahatta, draining into the inlets located along the Island's northwest coast; to those where isolation and solitude are the norm by venturing to the classified rivers such as the Ahnuhati, Kakweiken, Kingcome, Seymour and Wakeman rivers, located at the heads of inlets across on the mainland.

I remember vividly the trip that Van Egan and I made to the Wakeman River in April 1992, not so much for the fishing, although we did find steelhead, dollies and cutthroat in the Wakeman and chinooks in the sea, but because it ended up being a trip on which I may have saved my friend's life.

About halfway along our six-mile drift, Chris Bennett, our guide, put us on shore so that he could hand-line the raft through a tricky piece of water. No sooner had I jumped back into the raft, and as Van and Chris were about to do the same, than the gravel bank collapsed. Looking upstream I saw Chris scurrying and climbing over the edge of the raft, but when I looked downstream all I could see was Van's head and shoulders bobbing above the water. I lunged and grabbed his wading jacket and managed to pull him on board. Van had fallen in near the end of a large swirling back eddy. He said afterward that the bank just disappeared, the raft slid away and he found that he could not touch bottom. Who knows what the undercurrents may have done if I had not been able to grab him. But we do know that trying to swim in waders, in 5.5 degree C (42 degree F) water, fully clothed while holding onto six or seven hundred dollars worth of fly fishing equipment is a daunting task. Fortunately, Steve Vesley was living at the old logging camp on the estuary and we drifted there with haste after draining Van's waders and wringing out some of his clothes. Vesley made Van some hot drinks and dried his clothes so that he was comfortable for the boat trip back to Bennett's place.

REGION 2: LOWER MAINLAND

This is where all the people live, but even with half of the province's 4 million people nestled in the Lower Fraser Valley there is some fine fly fishing. Region 2 borders the U.S.A. on the south and includes the watersheds tributary to the Lower Fraser up to Spuzzum and the watersheds draining into Georgia Strait as far north as Bute Inlet. Other than the east coast of Vancouver Island, this is the most accessible section of British Columbia's mainland coast, with a ferry and road network stretching past Lund, north of Powell River.

I am Vancouver-born and based and have probably spent more time fishing this region's waters than all others. Anglers have been experiencing the thrills of its winter and summer steelhead, rainbow and cutthroat trout, Dolly Varden and all the Pacific salmon for more than a century. The Coquihalla near

Hope has had fly fishers plodding its banks since the earliest of colonial days and is the birthplace of British Columbia steelhead fishing. Because of the increasing population, it is becoming more difficult to find good fishing with solitude in Region 2.

Nonetheless, one often forgets other people when a Coquihalla summer-run or Squamish winter-run steelhead is rushing out line; or a Harrison cutthroat has fallen for one of your silver-bodied minnow patterns; or a Skagit rainbow has taken your mayfly imitation and is leaping about with a frenzy to escape; or Lower Fraser or Harrison system sockeye, pink, chum or coho is madly seeking a path through the river currents in its escape attempt.

Winter fishing can prove difficult for the fly, but as spring approaches usually the river temperatures rise enough and the fly produces better. On the Vedder this past winter I managed to connect with steelhead on each trip. At 8:15 one morning, I had a good tussle lasting a minute or so before the hook came away. Later, I decided to give the Quarry Run a shot. Below the run, the river shoots down a small set of rapids to a rock promontory, not passable to anglers. The fish felt good when I set the hook and it stayed in the gut for a while before it decided that the route to freedom lay downstream. I had read somewhere that one technique to stop a fish from heading down river required throwing a bunch of slack line to the current so that the pull comes from below. The fish is supposed to react to the now-downstream pull and swim upriver. Skeptical I was, but with no choice of following the fish down around the rock outcropping, I tried it. It worked and after 10 minutes or so I slid a large 37½-inch (95-cm) male steelhead onto the beach. As I removed my #2 General Practitioner from its jaw and slid the steelhead back into the water, I mused, what a grand fish the winter steelhead is to take on a fly, especially a fish as large from this the most heavily fished steelhead river in the province.

As this region is heavily populated, fly fishers must expect to share the waters with other anglers of other gear persuasions, particularly on weekends. Yet, this is a big region with the more northern parts quite remote. Heavily fished waters may be less crowded through the week, and in the more remote locations, if solitude is a prerequisite, it can be found.

REGION 3: THOMPSON—NICOLA

Region 3 encompasses the watersheds contributing to the Fraser River from Spuzzum north almost to the Gang Ranch, including the major tributary flowing from the east, the Thompson. This region is synonymous with lake fishing. More fly fishers from different parts of the province, North America and the world have probably, over the past century, cast their flies into such famous lakes as Lac Le Jeune, Knouff, Paul, Pinantan and Hyas and more recently White, Tunkwa, Leighton, Roche, Peterhope, Salmon, Stump, Island, Corbett, Minnie, Stoney and many others, than in the rest of the regions combined.

Most of British Columbia's coastal streams and lakes tend to be acidic. As a result, they do not support large quantities of insect life, and fish from those waters tend to be small. Rivers such as the Cowichan and Skagit are the exception. Most fish in coastal streams are anadromous. Anadromous fish return to fresh water on their spawning run, but as small fish they journey to the sea where they grow big. However, the opposite is true for many waters in Region 3. Some have the right mix of minerals such as calcium, phosphorous and nitrogen, which in turn provide the nutrients for water-dwelling insects to thrive and provide plenty of food for trout to grow large.

Insects such as freshwater shrimp, chironomids, mayfly, damselfly and dragonfly nymphs and leeches are found in great number in the various waters. Some of those populations need to be seen to be believed.

I remember one morning in May a few years back when a hatch of chironomids came off Tunkwa Lake. You had to keep your mouth shut to avoid breathing them in they were so thick. With insect life so bountiful and providing trout with so much choice, catching fish poses challenges. Nonetheless, where there is plentiful fish food, you will have fast-growing, good-sized trout, and anglers will devise flies and techniques to catch them. The chironomid techniques developed on Tunkwa (described in more detail later) are testimony to fly fishers' resourcefulness.

Whichever the water, a fly fisher needs to have in his or her arsenal of ies patterns representative of local fauna. Brian Chan, a Region 3 fisheries biologist and prominent stillwater fly fisher wrote *Flyfishing Strategies for Stillwaters* (1991). This book is a must read for those wanting to know more about catching stillwater trout.

Region 3 may be famous for its stillwater rainbow trout fishery, but fly fishers have been casting flies and catching trout in rivers along the Canadian Pacific Railway mainline since the building of the railway, completed in 1886. Streams such as the Thompson, south of Savona, and the Adams and Little are world-class fly fishing streams.

The Adams and Little rivers are unique fisheries because of the salmon that return to the Adams to spawn. On cycle years, sockeye return in the millions, and when the fry emerge from the gravel, trout, as they have for many millennia, lie in wait. For close to a century anglers, too, have eagerly awaited the fry emergence and seduced trout with their silver-bodied fry imitations. The Thompson is the only classified water in Region 3 and has fine rainbow trout fly fishing as well as some of largest, hardest-fighting summer-run steelhead in the world.

Two fellow members of the Totem Flyfishers walked out of the Thompson River's Y Pool corner one November evening. We had no takes but, as dusk was approaching fast, I did not want to be away too long from my son and his friend back at the camper, so I decided to spend the twilight minutes here. Over the years I have learned the intricacies of fishing this water and fished it with confidence, armed with the knowledge that fish like to lie in certain spots at certain heights.

On this November evening, I waded into the corner and, no sooner had I got into position and started casting than I had a good pull. It did not come back immediately so I thought I would finish the corner and come back and try again. I worked my way a little further down and was taken again. This time the fish was well hooked, and I could tell from the way the line came from my big Hardy Perfect reel that this fish had power and was a big steelhead. In total darkness and well down the run I slid a 39-inch- (99-cm-) plus male steelhead on the beach, my largest steelhead to the fly from that river up to that time.

Other fish besides rainbows that are common in the region include brook trout, Dolly Varden, lake trout, whitefish, kokanee, spring, coho, sockeye and, in some waters of the Fraser, sea-run cutthroat.

REGION 4: KOOTENAY

Few fly fishers know that British Columbia's first fly was dressed in this region when the boundary commission surveyed British Columbia's border with the United States in the 1860s. Few fly fishers also know that it was in Region 4 that the dry fly was used to catch trout in 1887, a North American first. (More on those two tidbits of British Columbia fly fishing lore are included in the history section.)

Region 4 borders the United States in the south and Alberta in the east. All of the waters in this region are part of the Columbia River Basin. However, fly fishers will not feel the surge of salmon pulling line from the reel. The once-prolific runs of Pacific salmon that called the upper Columbia watershed home have long become extinct because of the large dams constructed in the United States, which are not passable to fish. Nonetheless, fly fishers venturing into this region can expect to catch Westslope cutthroat, rainbows, bull trout, kokanee, bass and whitefish.

One September, I had a call from an angling acquaintance. The call centered mainly on the foreword I had written for his upcoming reprint of Dr. T. W. Lambert's classic 1907 book, *Fishing in British Columbia*, but like most fishermen's conversations, it soon turned to fishing. A biologist doing research work, he related some bull trout fly fishing that he had recently experienced on the Lardeau River. "Fish over 20 pounds [9 kg] that really hit the fly," he said, "and the large bucktail-type flies outfished the traditional spoon three or four to one." For many years, from 1932 to 1977, Knouff Lake boasted the province's largest stillwater dry fly-caught rainbow; however, in 1977 Tom Durkop topped that record with his 25 lb-2 oz (11.8 kg) monster from Kootenay Lake.

This is one of the regions in which I have not wetted a line. Even though it has some large-fish opportunities, they are mostly for trollers. But the above stories are living proof that big fish can be taken with a fly in this region. Every time I pick up a paper and read the fishing hints there is usually mention of the very good rainbow trout fly fishing to be had on the Lower Columbia. This time, one of the U.S. dams helped improve the fishery as trout venture out of the lake into the river in search of food and on their spawning run. Through management techniques such as catch-and-release and fly-fishing-only regulations, the cutthroat and rainbow fisheries on the St. Mary's River have been brought back and are now a destination for many fly fishers.

This is a large area with many lakes and rivers and, indeed, the fly fisher will be rewarded with a variety of experiences as he or she explores the waters of Region 4.

REGION 5: CARIBOO

For years the big-name lakes of Region 3 attracted visiting fly fishers, but as the Cariboo country opened up and fly fishers explored its waters, many became converts.

Region 5 includes the waters tributary to the Fraser River west of the Thompson watershed, from the Gang Ranch north to the watershed of the Blackwater (West Road) River and west to the sea at Bella Coola. Some fly fishers consider the lakes in the Chilcotin Plateau the finest small lake fly fishery in British Columbia. Lake fly fishers could spend months in this region exploring different lakes and streams.

I have vacationed in the Cariboo Region for the past 20 years and thrown flies into Quesnel, Hen Ingram, Klinne, Keno, Jacques, Raven and Palmer lakes and Canim, Atnarko, Bella Coola and Dean rivers. In those waters, of all the region's gamefish—rainbow, cutthroat, summer-run and winter-run steelhead, Dolly Varden, lake trout, coho, chinook, kokanee and bull trout—only the bull trout has evaded my flies. The bull trout's reclassification, which separated inland char from coastal Dolly Varden, is recent. Perhaps, some of those dollies I caught in Region 5 over the years were in fact bull trout.

This region is home to some of the province's finest waters, and many, such as the Atnarko, Bella Coola, Chilcotin, Chilko, Dean, Kilbella, Nekite and West Road/Blackwater, have classified waters designation.

Anglers venture from all over the world to test their skill with the Dean

River summer-run steelhead. This river has one of the last wilderness wild runs of summer steelhead that respond oh-so-well to the fly. Dean steelhead make angling legends. However, for the river trout fly fisher, the upper Dean below Anahim Lake and the Blackwater, another world-class stream, have much to offer. Cutthroat fly fishers in search of the sea-runs have experienced amazing fishing in rivers such as the Bella Coola when the salmon fry migration is on.

Many of my sojourns into this region have been in pursuit of steelhead. From 1983 through to the early 1990s, Gary Baker and I took fishing vacations here with our sons. Often we were joined by other fathers and their kids, and my son usually brought along a friend. From those vacations I have many fond memories.

My son Charles (or "C.T." as we call him) was due to turn six years old in a couple of weeks and I wondered about taking him so far away from home and his mother. But there would be other kids—Gary's son Drew and Drew's cousin Ryan—camping with us.

This was my son's first trip away fishing with me, and when we started he wanted me to do the fishing, even though I explained to him what was involved. I did not press the point and over the next day or so he watched us fish, sometimes with me or in Gary's boat with the other boys. However, with the enthusiasm that Drew and Ryan showed I could see C.T.'s interest increase. He did the smart thing: watch the old man and others, learn, and then when he felt confident that he could catch fish, he went for it. His first five trout that he caught himself on a trolled Doc Spratley ranged from 1¼–1¾ lb (0.5–0.8 kg)—not bad for a little guy.

Since that first trip we have enjoyed many other fishing vacations in Region 5. This region is an excellent place for family fishing excursions: a little farther to travel but plenty of fine waters.

REGION 6: SKEENA

When fly fishers talk Skeena country, rivers such as the Kispiox, Bulkley, Morice, Babine and Sustat and their summer-run steelhead are usually the topic.

The Kispiox holds two distinctions in British Columbia steelhead angling history: the largest rod-caught and the largest fly-caught summer-run steelhead both came from this river. Chuck Ewart took the rod-caught world record 36-lb (16-kg) steelhead in the 1950s and Karl Mausser the world-record fly-caught, a 33-pounder (15-kg) in 1962.

The name Skeena is perhaps not the best descriptor for this vast region. Although the region contains the waters tributary to the mighty Skeena and an angler could spend all his days fishing the waters of that great watershed, it also includes the Kitimat and Kitlope watersheds to the southeast and a portion of the Fraser watershed south of Burns Lake. Furthermore, the area north of the Skeena watershed, which is as large as or larger than the southern portion of the region, includes the Nass, Stikine and other watersheds whose rivers flow through the Alaska Panhandle. Some waters in the very north, including British Columbia's largest natural lake, Atlin, whose waters cross the Yukon border, flow into the Arctic Ocean. Off the west coast lie the Queen Charlotte Islands, a delight to fish.

Skeena is known as big-fish country and fly fishers are attracted by its trophy-sized steelhead and huge chinook salmon. I have a friend living in Terrace who talks of 50-pound (22.5-kg) chinooks taken on a fly. Coho, pink, chum and sockeye all promise the fly fisher adventure in many of the waters flowing to the sea along Region 6's coast. Fly fishers searching for rainbow, cutthroat and Dolly Varden should not overlook rivers such as the Kitimat, Lakelse and other tributaries, as well as the many lakes of the mainland. The rivers tributary to the Arctic drainage system offer pike and Arctic grayling.

One of the jewels of the region is the Queen Charlotte Islands. On the Islands, fly fishers enjoy catching most species of salmon, winter steelhead and sea-run cutthroat in rivers such as the Tlell, Copper and Yakoun, and cutthroat in lakes such as Skidegate, Yakoun and Mosquito.

With 26 classified rivers, this region has more specially designated waters than any other in the province. Fly fishers wanting to experience some of the finest fly fishing in the world can find quality fishing to match one's budget, from $500-a-day-or-more lodges with guides to run you around in boats or helicopter you to remote waters, to camping in the wilderness and doing it all yourself. Whichever suits your budget, you will find adventure and take home fond memories from a trip to this region.

After spending a couple of weeks on the Queen Charlottes Islands with my 12-year-old son and his friend catching cutthroat trout and pink salmon, I put the boys on the same plane going to Vancouver that Bob Taylor had arrived on. Bob and I headed across to the mainland to fish the streams around Terrace. The steelheading was not as good as it could have been, but I was pleased with the large 35-inch (89 cm) I took, and the dollies to 20 in (51 cm) that came often enough to my Black Spey fly were a bonus. For a change, and before we started on our long journey home, we drove over the divide to the Kitimat to try for cutthroat. That day we were into two dozen cutthroat, with Taylor's 19 incher (48 cm) the largest. As we journeyed home with memories of dollies, cutts, coho, pinks and summer-run steelhead, I was struck by how much the Skeena region has to offer. Even then, we had only scratched the surface.

REGION 7: OMINECA—PEACE

This region includes probably the largest area of unsettled lands in the province. It stretches from south of Prince George north to the Yukon and Northwest Territories boundary and to Alberta on the east. Prince George is the jumping-off place, and fly fishers heading into Region 7 for adventure have three highways from which to choose. Highway 16 northwest takes you into the upper northwest portions of the Fraser watershed, to the fishing waters around Vanderhoof, Fort St. James, Fraser Lake, and then into the waters of the Skeena Country, in Region 6. However, if you turn east at Prince George, Highway 16 takes you into southeast section of the Fraser watershed to the waters around McBride and Valemount in the shadows of the Rocky Mountains.

Carry north on Highway 97 and you will wind your way through all the north country, passing towns in the Peace River watershed such as Mackenzie, Chetwynd, Dawson Creek, Fort St. John and Fort Nelson, joining up with Highway 37, the Stewart—Cassiar Highway, just north of the Yukon border west of Watson Lake. Most of the streams in this region, north along High-way 97 (here called the Alaska Highway), with the exception of portions mentioned that are tributary to the Fraser watershed, are tributary to the Arctic Ocean.

Anglers can expect to find, besides the rainbow and cutthroat trout, Dolly Varden, bull trout, brook trout, lake trout, chars, whitefishes, and pike and grayling, the fishes of the Arctic drainage.

Anglers venturing north into Region 7 will enjoy the region's unique geography, from the huge-lake district around Fort St. James, to the flat grasslands of the Peace River country, to the scrub forest and muskeg in the northern parts of the region.

The Stellako, with its quality rainbow trout fishing, is the only classified water in this vast area. But that should not deter fly fishers from venturing into and exploring Region 7, especially if the goal is to find different fish in different settings and enjoy solitude.

One of my ambitions in the next few years, after I retire, is to take the ferry from Port Hardy near the north end of Vancouver Island in Region 1 to Prince Rupert in Region 6, transfer to the Alaska State ferry and sail to Skagway, then drive back, fishing the northern waters of Region 6 and 7 along the way.

REGION 8: OKANAGAN

Lake country—that is what I think about when I hear the name Okanagan. Trout-filled it was, and Matthew MacFie in *Vancouver Island and British Columbia* (1865) provides early testimonial to the numbers of fish in Okanagan Lake. He writes that "they may be taken out with nets in wagon-loads, and by wading in the water one may catch them with the hand without difficulty."

Sandwiched as it is between Regions 2, 3 and 5, and out of the influence of coastal weather patterns, summer vacationers flock to Region 8 to enjoy its desert-like climate. Fly fishers bound to ry their luck in this region will find that the trout are not quite as abundant nor as big as the pioneers found them, but they will find some pleasant lakes to fish in this the province's smallest region.

The rivers from the northern part of the region around Armstrong and east of Vernon are tributary to the Thompson watershed, while the waters draining the remainder are all part of the Columbia watershed.

Besides rainbow trout, flyfishers will find Westslope cutthroat and brown trout; Dolly Varden, bull, lake and brook trout char, and largemouth and small-mouth bass.

Fly fishers will find angling opportunities from spring through fall, but during the hot months of summer the best bet is the high-altitude lakes in the mountains surrounding and separating the various valleys in the region.

It was early summer and the weather was good, so when we accepted the invitation to visit my boyhood friend at his ranch in the Princeton area, I knew that socializing with family and friends would take precedence over fishing. Nonetheless, I reasoned that I might be able to squeeze in a little lake fishing. The lake, rich in aquatic life, had some good trout, with the largest pulling the scales to 14 lb (6 kg).

I decided not to take the boat and wandered along the shore. Spooking some nice rainbows that were in the shallows shrimping, I cast my Dark Olive Carey Special over the shore-reeds into deeper water. Four fish came to the fly that morning and the two that I took weighed 5 and 6 lb (2.3 and 2.7 kg).

I have had many enjoyable trips into the Okanagan Region over the past 20 years and look forward to many more.

Fly Fishing History

British Columbia's fly fishing roots go back to the earliest of our colonial days. After the colonies of Vancouver Island and British Columbia were established, many of the British who came to administer the affairs of the colonial governments were fly fishers and, of course, they introduced their British fly fishing techniques to the fishes they found. The steelhead, cutthroat and rainbows of lake and stream, and coho salmon in the sea responded quite well to their flies and fishing techniques. The colonial anglers wrote home and let family and friends know of the sport available in this new land, and those promising reports induced others to come. They, too, explored the waters of this little-populated land and many recorded their catches in the books they wrote, documenting their travels. Scarce titles such as John Keast Lord's *The Naturalist in British Columbia* (1865), H. W. Seton-Karr's *Bear-Hunting in the White Mountains or Alaska and British Columbia Revisited* (1891), and Dr. T. W. Lambert's *Fishing in British Columbia* (1907) are but a few of many written from 1865 to early in the 1900s, before the First World War, that provide testimonials to the sport they found.

American-born John Pease Babcock came to British Columbia to work as Deputy Commissioner of Fisheries. His book *The Game Fishes of British Columbia* (1908) is the first pictorial essay on the province's fishing opportunities. After living and sampling the fishing in British Columbia since 1895, Arthur Bryan Williams documented the province's fishing opportunities in *Rod and Creel in British Columbia* (1919), and later in *Fishing in British Columbia* (1935), and in both treatises he summarized the established fly fishing techniques and flies of the day.

From about 1910 on into the 1950s Lower Mainland fly fishers such as Frank Darling, Paul Moody Smith and Bill Cunliffe carried on the traditions of earlier fly fishers and introduced other fly fishing techniques as they searched with their dry and wet flies for the Capilano summer-run steelhead, and with their wet flies for the coho salmon and cutthroat of the Capilano, Harrison, Stave and Nicomekl rivers. The legendary steelhead fly fisher General Noel Money came to Vancouver Island in 1913 to fish tyee at Campbell River and decided to stay, building his home at Qualicum Beach. After he returned from service in World War I, he fished Stamp River summer-run and Somass winter-run steelhead. In later years he was mentor to the young Roderick Haig-Brown who, in turn, documented the steelhead fly fishing techniques the General and he used in his B.C. classic, *The Western Angler* (1939). Haig-Brown and Money, along with other steelhead fly fishers, laid foundations for following generations of steelhead fly fishers to build on Disciples such as Martin Tolley, Bob Taylor, Denny Boulton and Jerry Wintle carried on the traditions of Haig-Brown, Money, Tommy Brayshaw and other pioneer steelhead fly fishers, passing on their knowledge to anglers of my generation.

Haig-Brown, Money, Darling, Smith and Cunliffe also pursued the coastal cutthroat that abounded in rivers and creeks along coastal British Columbia. The flies and techniques they employed work well today.

One fishery that made British Columbia famous and attracted anglers from many places on the globe was the lake fly fishing of the Interior around Kamloops. Fish Lake, later renamed Lac Le Jeune in honour of Father Le Jeune, a missionary who worked with the Shuswap native people around the turn of the century, gave up a catch of 1,500 trout to Dr. T. W. Lambert and his companion in 1897. Other lakes in the area were to become more famous.

European settlers noticed that many lakes were barren of trout, yet had prolific aquatic life, so starting in 1908 with Paul and Pinantan lakes, they packed fingerling trout to some lakes and released then. Within five years of their stockings, fly fishers experienced on lakes such as Paul, Pinantan, Hyas and Knouff fish in the 15–20-lb (7–9-kg) range on both wet and dry flies. In the 1920s, A. Bryan Williams developed the first sedge dry flies for interior lake fly fishing. However, it was the legendary guru, Bill Nation—guide, fly developer and angler—with whom anglers from around the globe came to fish. Nation based his guiding operation from Paul Lake, and his clients fished Paul and the surrounding waters, enjoying those marvelous fish and legendary sedge dry fly fishing. Fly fishers of today still eagerly await the sedge dry fly fishing that Williams established and Nation promoted. Often the sedge fishing is the highlight of an Interior trout fly fisher's year.

No fly fishing history would be complete without the mention of the ardent angler, artist and fly tyer, Tommy Brayshaw, another British immigrant. During the 1920s and 1930s, Brayshaw, besides enjoying the dry and wet fly fishing in Knouff and other lakes, became a regular at the Adams and Little rivers, where he refined the fly fishing techniques and developed fly patterns for that unique world-class river fishery. In 1947 Brayshaw moved to Hope, where he became the pre-eminent steelhead fly fisherman on the Coquihalla. His Coquihalla series of steelhead flies is testimony to his love of that river and its summer-run steelhead.

Money, Haig-Brown, Brayshaw, William, Darling, Smith and Nation all are part of the golden age of B.C. fly fishing. Indeed, 1960s fly fishers like Martin Tolley, Jim Kilburn, John Massey, Bob Taylor, Jerry Wintle, Van Egan, Bill Yonge, Tom Murray, Barry Thornton, Ken Ruddick, Jack Shaw and others all owe them a debt. Likewise do fly fishers such as Rob Brown, Peter Caverhill, Jack Morris, Ehor Boyanowsky, Alf Davy, Brian Chan, Jim Fisher, Karl Bruhn, Ron Nelson, Ian Forbes, Rory Glennie, Brian Smith and others of around my generation plus or minus a few years, owe a debt to them. And so it is that each generation passes on the traditions of theirs and past generations to the next generation of fly fishers. And so it will be as long as we have places to fish and fish to catch.

When you look back over the past century or so and examine British Columbia's fly fishing history, you begin to understand that this place called British Columbia is unique and offers a tremendous amount to the fly fisher. Some of the notable British Columbia fly fishing achievements:

- John Keast Lord developed first fly for B.C. trout in the 1860s.
- Lees and Clutterbuck introduced the dry fly to North America during their 1887 exploration of the upper Columbia River.
- Bryan Williams developed B.C.'s first sedge dry flies for the sedge fishing on Interior lakes during the 1920s.
- Bill Nation introduced or refined lake fly fishing techniques and produced North America's first imitations of lake fauna such as dragonfly nymphs and chironomids during the 1920s.
- British Columbia saltwater fly fishers introduce bucktails and establish saltwater fly fishing techniques at Cowichan and Duncan Bays on Vancouver Island during the 1920s.
- Capilano River fly fishers Frank Darling, Austin Spencer, and Paul Moody Smith introduced or practiced dry fly fishing for steelhead and Austin Spencer produced North America's first steelhead dry fly during the 1920s.
- Greased (floating) line Atlantic salmon technique introduced to summer-run steelhead by Rod Haig-Brown and General Noel Money during the late 1930s.

- Bill Nation used greased (floating) line technique for presenting flies to Interior trout during the late 1930s.
- Chironomid fly fishing techniques developed for interior lakes and refined into a must-use technique by a variety of anglers during the late 1960s.
- From 1920s through to the present day B.C. fly fishers produce a myriad of fly patterns for cutthroat, steelhead, interior rainbow and salmon.

Each achievement is testimony to British Columbia fly fishers and the opportunities offered in this vast land of opportunity.

Wilderness, Wild Animals, Bugs and First Aid

If British Columbia's four million people were scattered evenly throughout the province the density would be 11 persons per square mile. However, most live in the southerly part close to the coast, with about two million living in the Lower Fraser Valley and another half million or so along the east coast of Vancouver Island. Many of the remaining million plus people live in towns and villages scattered throughout the province south of Prince George. With most of the population settled in specific regions, British Columbia is mostly wilderness and remains the domain of wild animals.

When we make our sojourns out of our urban environments into the wilderness we must keep that in mind. You need not go far out of the urban areas to see wildlife.

Urban dwellers venturing into wilderness country often fear animal encounters. If the truth be known, people are in probably in more danger in their urban environment with more chance of being hurt by fellow humans that they ever would be by animals out in the wilderness. Yet that unease exists probably because it is a change from their normal experience, and camping out in the wilderness does take some getting used to. Usually I sleep in a recreational vehicle, but I remember how fitful my sleep was with having only the thin canvas walls of a tent protecting me from black and grizzly bears on my first trip to the Dean River in 1983.

British Columbia has a wide variety of indigenous animals and it is not uncommon to see many during any given vacation in the wilderness. Chipmunks, squirrels, groundhogs, marmots, weasels, beaver, otters, raccoons, coyotes, skunks, voles, mice and other small animals are fairly common. Some of these share our urban settings. At work one of our supervisors sought a permit from the Ministry of Environment to capture some beavers that were damming an urban waterway in Burnaby. One morning while driving to work I saw a coyote two blocks from my home.

Out of the urban settings, driving along highways and on secondary roads or while hiking you can see deer, elk, moose, black or grizzly bears, and occasionally you might see foxes, wolves, coyotes, big horn sheep and mountain goat, but animals such as lynx and cougars are rarely seen. In all my years I have seen one lynx and one cougar, although I have witnessed cougar prints in the snow while fishing along rivers in winter. What animals you may see depends on the region you happen to be in, but because of our activity—fishing—we need to pay particular attention to *ursus americanus and ursus artos horribilis*—the black and grizzly bears.

Black bears are common throughout the province, including all coastal islands, while the grizzly inhabits only the mainland. Black bears are not as seriously affected by human encroachment into their habitat as are grizzlies, which require a pristine environment. Grizzlies have been driven from many areas of the province due to resource exploitation and urban settlement.

I like to see bears. They are the highlight of many fishing excursions. But I like to view them from a distance. They are large animals whose search for food is foremost and they will follow their noses. I remember back a few years when Bob Taylor and I were camped in a small meadow, that we later referred to as Bear Meadow, not far from the Copper River's Clore tributary, near Terrace. I have an old camper with a loose door and just after we climbed out of bed we heard what at first sounded like someone tapping on the door. I asked Bob if he had heard anyone drive in as it was pretty early in the morning. "No," he said, as he poked his head through the door curtain, spying a black bear not far away. The bear did seem to be frightened by us. In fact, it sauntered up to the truck door and pawed and sniffed at the window. Dressing quickly, I went out to shoo it away, but it took its time and appeared not at all alarmed by my presence. Eventually, it sauntered off to eat some berries from a nearby bush. After the bear was far enough away, I went up to the truck cab to see if his pawing damaged the paint. I noticed a small bag of garbage sitting on the floor of the cab. We had driven in from Prince Rupert the day before and had intended to get rid of our garbage at one of the many highway garbage containers, but we forgot. The bear must have caught a whiff of that sweet-smelling garbage and followed its nose to the camper. The tap-tap we had heard was it pawing at the back door in search of the source of that smell.

When humans panic or are not careful, sometimes bear encounters like those culminate in disaster. When fishing or camping in bear country follow these precautions:

- Hang your food high in the trees or store in a vehicle or camper.
- Do not leave food in a tent or tent trailer.
- Clean fish well away from camp.
- Bury fish guts well away from camp.
- Wash your hands after cleaning fish and wipe them clean.
- Keep your clothing odour free.
- Burn garbage including tin cans to get rid of food odours.
- Be aware and look for fresh bear signs such as droppings, prints and claw marks on trees.
- When you see a bear give it a wide berth, particularly a mother with cubs.
- Remember, bears do not want to run into you any more than you want to bump into them. When hiking to fishing spots, make your presence known by talking with your companion or making other noise.

Wilderness and wild animals are to be enjoyed. We can show how we value both by respecting the wild animals that live there and by taking all our garbage with us, leaving the wilderness the way we found it.

Insects are undoubtedly more of a nuisance than most wild animals, although mice can be a pest if they get into food. Mosquitoes, horseflies, no-see-ums (midges), deer flies and wasps are everywhere. The quantity and degree that you will find them a nuisance is often dependent on the time of your visit and the weather. Each summer I go to the Dean, and on those hot midsummer days the horseflies can be a real nuisance, even out on the river. If you prepare food for cooking out of doors, wasps will be attracted to the food and can be quite a pest, although generally they will not sting you unless they feel threatened.

One summer on the Dean, wasps were everywhere. They loved to drink the nectar from around a pop tin, often exploring inside. I tapped my tin to shoo away the wasps sitting on top and listened for any buzzing inside. Hearing no noise I took a sip. Fortunately the wasp inside was more shocked than I and I managed to spit it out before it stung me. Such incidents could be painful, so beware of black-striped, yellow-bodied insects around your food or drink.

On the cooler days and evenings, mosquitoes and black flies are the nuisance, and after a rain, no-see-ums. During a June trip to the Cowichan after a lengthy period of rainy weather, we camped at Skutz Falls on the evening that the weather started to improve. The damp, humid and warming environment proved ideal for insects, and the no-see-ums found every crack, invading the camper in such numbers that we could not get to sleep. My son had his car there so we got out of bed, dressed, lit a mosquito coil in the camper and went for a 45-minute drive in his car. When we returned, the fumes from the coil had done their job and the evening had cooled enough that no new no-see-ums were around.

Make sure when you venture off into the woods that you have bug repellent, mosquito coils and, if allergic to bug bites, antihistamines (consult your physician). Bob Taylor, a longtime angling acquaintance, swells up badly when he gets bitten by an insect. Antihistamines are the magic medicine that allows him to be safe in the bush.

Besides precautions to deter the bugs, you should have a first-aid kit to treat the odd cut, bruise, insect bite or, on those very hot days when you stay out too long, sunburn. Furthermore, hooks inevitably now and then become imbedded in human flesh. Once the hook is removed the damaged area should be sterilized and bandaged. I wear sunglasses most of the time to protect my eyes from wayward flies. I recall a few times taking hooks out of my body and those of friends. Humans getting in the way of flies reminds me of my "Dr. Bob" story.

I saw the guide boat speeding up the river, which seemed odd. It was mid-morning, prime fishing time, and it had not been that long since the guide had gone down river with his client, so I figured something was up. The boat pulled in above where I was fishing and the guide dropped back and asked if I knew where Bob Taylor happened to be. I said, "Up at the Fir Pool," and away they sped.

I talked with Bob later and he said that the guide's client had hooked himself in the face and the only person the client would let remove the hook was Bob Taylor. Taylor obliged, easily removing the barbless hook. Why Taylor? Apparently, when we flew from Vancouver to the Dean River, Bob had chatted with this American from Seattle about many things. Taylor has fly fished for over four decades and is a good conversationalist who can cover a wide range of subjects during a two-hour flight. Something Bob had said during the flight had impressed this fellow so much that he would let no one other than Bob attempt to dislodge the hook. No, Bob is not a doctor, but now whenever we talk about the incident we refer to Taylor as "Dr. Bob." If there is a moral to that story, it is this: Be prepared when venturing into the wilderness. Chances of finding a Dr. Bob will be slim, and you will need to look after yourself and your companions.

CHAPTER TWO
The Game Fishes of British Columbia

There are few places in the world where fish played a part in determining territories. It happened here in British Columbia. When Vancouver Island and, later, British Columbia were colonized, little was known about the sporting qualities of our native game fish. Most encounters with salmon took place in the ocean, and comparisons were quickly made to the Atlantic salmon of the European continent, whose qualities as a game fish for fly fishers reigned supreme.

In the mid 1800s, it was commonly believed that Pacific salmon would not take the fly. Indeed, it was also rumoured that England's Foreign Secretary of the 1840s, Lord Aberdeen (on the advice of his brother-in-law, Captain John Gordon, who had actually fished for Pacific salmon), suggested giving Washington and Oregon to the Americans to avoid war. The territory was evidently not considered worth fighting for simply because the Pacific salmon would not take the fly. Clearly, Captain Gordon was not impressed with the country he saw or with the methods used for catching Pacific salmon. He concluded that he would not give "the most barren hills in the Highlands of Scotland" for all he saw on the Pacific Coast.

Despite Captain Gordon's unfavourable report, in ensuing years other

British travelers came, sampled our fly fishing and took away quite different stories. About the fishing for Vancouver Island's steelhead and sea-run cutthroat, F. G. Aflalo in *Sunset Playgrounds* (1909), writes,

> For the fisherman Vancouver Island is holy ground by reason of the splendid sport obtainable with steelhead trout in the Cowichan River. This is a long journey from Victoria, but even here, in the city, is a park, known as The Gorge, in which it is possible to catch sea-trout on the fly in salt-water, a chance surely all but unique in all the eleven-and-a-half million square miles of the British Empire.

Later, in the same chapter, he mentions his trip to Kamloops and the rainbows of Fish Lake (Lac Le Jeune) and praises highly the trout fishing around Kamloops and the rainbow's fighting qualities. He writes:

> ...the angler with time to spare may fish half-a-dozen lakes in which the trout-fishing, wonderful, as I am about to describe, in the worst of them improves in direct [proportion to the] inaccessibility of each from Kamloops....the trout run very large, and are almost too plentiful for good sport....At the very first cast I hooked two, one of close on two pounds, the other half a pound less. These lake rainbows jump like tarpon six or eight times, and they fight like demons.

I could not find a more fitting passage to introduce the rainbow trout than those remarks made by Aflalo nearly a century ago. British Columbia's fly fishers have about a dozen and a half game fish that can be taken by the fly. I am going to use common names. It only confuses the issue to deal with scientific nomenclature. For example, fisheries scientists recently reclassified our native trouts from the genus *Salmo*—the group that contains the Atlantic salmon—to *Oncorhynchus*—the group that contains the Pacific salmon. If common names followed suit, we would be calling the rainbow trout a rainbow salmon. Common names, often quite descriptive and usually unique, have been around since anglers first cast their flies on and into the water and fish found them appealing. However, the same fish may have different common names in different locations and regions. I will use those referred to in the angling regulations with perhaps cursory mention of others used locally.

RAINBOW TROUT

For something to become legendary it must possess certain appealing attributes. Indeed, it was the rainbow trout fly fishing found in the Interior of B.C. that made the rainbow trout legendary. The earlier fly fishers' reports from the Thompson and Little rivers and Lac Le Jeune, supplemented by those in the mid-to-late 1920s through the 1940s from legendary lakes such as Knouff, Pinantan and Hyas where big, silver-bright, high-leaping, hard-fighting fish and plenty of them came readily to the fly, solidified in anglers' minds the rainbow's reputation as British Columbias premier fly fisher's fish.

The rainbow trout is a startlingly beautiful fish. It is often silver bright, but the colouration will vary depending on maturity, water conditions and diet. Many game fish take on quite different colouration during spawning. Rainbow trout spawn throughout the spring and become quite dark, with an enhanced rainbow stripe along the side.

Rainbows in varying degrees of colour can be caught from the same water, especially in the early part of the spring trout season. At first, when anglers caught these different-coloured specimens they were thought to be different fish. When professor David Starr Jordan, eminent North American fisheries scientist of the day, wrote *American Food and Game Fishes* (1908), he included no less than 10 species of rainbow and steelhead trout. Certainly in British Columbia, the most renowned local rainbow of Interior lakes was called the "Kamloops" trout. Even today some Interior anglers still refer to the rainbow as a "Kamloops" trout. However, the rainbow is a rainbow no matter what it is called, where it is caught or what it looks like. (The steelhead is the sea-going form and I will deal with it later.)

Most game fishes have a darker top and lighter bottom, and the colour change takes place along the lateral line, located mid-body. It is the pinkish to red colouration along this line that gives the rainbow trout its name. However, on some fish it is almost indistinguishable, occurring only as a pink hue sometimes restricted to gill covers or cheeks of the fish. The rainbow also has small black spots mostly restricted to its back above the lateral line and radiating rows of spots on the tail. Unlike the cutthroat, the rainbow trout has no teeth in the throat back of the tongue.

The rainbow trout is the most widely distributed game fish in the province and is found in all regions. The rainbow will vary in size, depending on age when caught and food supply where they live. The average rainbow trout will live about six years. Official and other records tell that the rainbow can attain weights into the 50-lb (22.5 kg) range. Jewel Lake in Region 8 northwest of Grand Forks produced huge fish in the 40–50-lb (18–22.5-kg) range during the 1930s and early 1940s. Alas, those giants are now only memories, but there are rainbows of various sizes in many waters of the province to test the fly fisher's prowess with a fly.

In lakes, fly-caught rainbows of 5–10 lb (2.3–4.5 kg) are considered trophy fish, with the occasional specimen going larger. (Rainbow in some of the large lakes such as Shuswap and Kootenay attain weights of 30 lb (13.5 kg), but mostly these are deep dwellers more easily caught trolling.) In rivers, fly-caught rainbows of 2–4 lb (0.9–1.8 kg) are trophy fish. However, on some Interior rivers where sockeye salmon spawn in large numbers, sockeye fry hatch in the millions and move to nearby lakes where the small fish rear for two years. During their lake residency and when they migrate toward the ocean as smolts, the young sockeye provide a ready supply of food. Rainbow trout feeding on a diet of small sockeye can grow big, with fish of 5–10 lb (2.3–4.5 kg) not uncommon and larger specimens occasionally being caught. Little River near Chase, Quesnel River near Williams Lake and Babine Lake near Topley can provide examples of the sockeye phenomenon.

STEELHEAD TROUT

This is another fish with an unusual handle. I wondered about the name's origin and spent nine months one year writing to museums and researching fisheries' papers, until I eventually found early written records. After finding reference to it in one of W. H. Seton-Carr's books, I dated the written use of "steelhead" in British Columbia back to 1891. However, the word was used 10 years earlier by American fisheries scientist Dr. David Starr Jordan, and I am confident that colloquial use goes back even further. In "Notes of the Fishes of the Pacific Coast of the United States," published in *Procedures of the United States National Museum, Volume IV, 1881* (1882) by David Starr Jordan and Charles H. Gilbert, under *Salmo gairdneri,* we find the first written attestation of the word "steelhead" and the other common name of the day, "hardhead." Jordan, who had done research on Fraser River fish in the 1870s, mistakenly placed the steelhead in with the trout later to be called the cutthroat, but at that time classified as *Salmo purpuratus.* Jordan claimed that steelhead and hardhead were the common names used for this fish by the market fishermen along the coast.

The steelhead is a sea-going rainbow trout. It spawns and the offspring rear from one to three or four years in fresh water, depending on available food and growing season, before migrating to the ocean where they grow to a large size. When the steelhead returns to the river it has a steely blue dorsal surface, silvery sides with black spots on back, dorsal fin and tail. As it continues to mature sexually after entering fresh water, it takes on the tell-tale colouration of its rainbow ancestors. Females, after months in fresh water, may only show a slight tinge of pink on the cheeks and have a light rainbow hue along the lateral line. Males colour much more, and more quickly. Steelhead can range greatly in size from about 2 to over 30 lb (0.9–13.5 kg). A 5-lb (2.3-kg) steelhead is a small fish in British Columbia and any fish 15 lb (7 kg) and larger is a good-sized fish in most rivers.

Steelhead populations vary in abundance from year to year and are small compared to salmon populations, which number in the thousands and tens of thousands, with some sockeye and pink populations returning to their home rivers in the millions. Steelhead, on the other hand, generally number in the hundreds, with only a few stocks returning in the thousands. To illustrate, before interceptions the Thompson with three main stocks has a run of

6–10,000; the Skeena, with about five stocks, 50–75,000, and the Chilliwack with one stock, 6–8,000.

In the mid-1980s we experienced large runs, perhaps larger than the runs I remember of late 1960s and certainly larger than any in the previous decade. Steelhead returns all along the coast were phenomenal as was the fishing. However, like all cyclic things, the low must come, and it is with us now. There is fear, though, that the lows we now experience have been caused by decades of indiscriminate slaughter by market fishers, habitat destruction and the adverse effects of climate change and poor ocean conditions. Steelhead populations may not rebound. I hope this is not so, but the warning signs are evident. In past years, returns to the Thompson in some seasons have been near the 900 minimum needed to sustain the stocks.

Steelhead can be caught year-round in the province if you are willing to travel to different locations, and I have taken them in 36 different rivers in every month but June. Although they are morphologically the same fish, steelhead can be put into two racial groups: winter-run and summer-run. The characteristics that distinguish one race from the other are the timing of river entry and sexual maturity at entry. Summer-run steelhead enter fresh water often hundreds of miles from their destination stream through May to early October, and all summer-runs are sexually immature. Winter-run steelhead enter fresh water usually from December to May in a far more advanced state of sexual maturity than their summer-run counterparts, which do most of their maturing in the river during winter and spring. Both races spawn in the spring following their freshwater entry.

Winter-Run: Around the beginning of winter, the first winter fish start to show in certain rivers. For example, the Yakoun on the Queen Charlotte Islands has fish returning from November through May, the Cowichan on Vancouver Island and Vedder on the Lower Mainland from December through May. Peak timing of a run is dependent on many factors, such as difficulty and length of journey to the spawning ground. Often on coastal rivers fish are drawn into that stream by the rains of winter. On some rivers like the Squamish or Wakeman, although they may have fish coming in as early as December, the bulk of the run is drawn in when the snow pack begins to melt, often in April or, if a late freshet, May. Those late-running winter fish are ready to spawn quickly.

Winter fish are found in all regions that border the coast. It was thought that Region 3 had some winter fish until radio tagging and tracking done in 1996–97 provided evidence that the steelhead returning to rivers along the Fraser such as the Nahatlach, Stein and Seton entered the Fraser along with Thompson fish and were summer-runs. Those fish held in the Fraser Canyon during winter and moved into the tributaries in late winter and early spring.

Winter steelhead fly fishing is tough. Water temperatures through most of the winter are around the 40 degree F (4.5 degree C) range, and often lower. Fish are not active takers in cold water. The fly fisher must go deep and dirty to be successful. To present the fly properly requires deep wading in cold water, and even neoprene waders are often inadequate insulators. However, as winter wanes, usually in March, water temperatures start to move up and fish become more active. Even then the fly fisher needs to probe deeply with his flies. An angler will wonder, when the fly stops on its swing, whether he has hooked bottom or a steelhead. Once the "bottom" moves, you will not know if it is a small steelhead or a 20-pounder (9 kg). No matter what size, any winter steelhead will leave you shaking with excitement as you play and land the fish. Fly fishers who work hard for winter fish will be rewarded.

Summer-Run: Anglers fishing world-renowned summer-run rivers such as the Thompson in Region 3 or the Kispiox, Babine, Bulkley and Sustut in Region 6 catch steelhead during the late summer and fall through until the rivers close to angling on December 31. These fish entered fresh water in the summer and early fall months.

Summer steelhead are very interesting because they have the unique capability to access and use habitat that is often not available to their winter-returning cousins. In some instances summer steelhead access river areas that no other species except bull trout (char) are able to reach. These fish make the migration at just the right time. They are able to maximize their own upstream performance since their energy reserves are optimal for strength and endurance. They are not yet hindered by the physiological changes needed for spawning, which can be as long as nine or 10 months away. The habitat they are seeking is often upstream from tough canyon chutes and drops and they encounter more favourable water and river-temperature conditions as river runoff subsides with the conclusion of the spring snow melt.

On small streams this can happen as early as May, but on the larger streams such as the Fraser and Skeena migration usually begins in late summer and continues through early fall. Steelhead are spring spawners and summer-runs return to the river with enough fat reserves to last them until the following spring when they must endure the rigours of spawning. A small percentage of steelhead survive spawning, return to the sea and, after regeneration, return to spawn again.

Summer-run steelhead are found in all coastal regions. Region 1 has a number of summer-run streams. Most are on the west coast of Vancouver Island. The Campbell River use to have a small run of summer steelhead that Roderick Haig-Brown recorded. Perhaps it was angling pressure and habitat degradation that affected the run's survival. However, about a dozen years ago some Tsitika River summer-runs were transplanted to the Campbell and many fly fishers now enjoy catching those fish on the river that Haig-Brown made famous. Tsitika stocks were used for the planting because the Tsitika, located up the coast a short distance, is the closest stream to the Campbell and it was believed that those fish may possess some of the same characteristics as the original Campbell stock.

Most Vancouver Island summer-run rivers are not big rivers and have small populations of summer steelhead. Region 2 has the Coquihalla River and Silverhope Creek at Hope, but with low steelhead populations in recent years, even catch-and-release fisheries have been curtailed on the Coquihalla. The Coquihalla has had years with less than 100 returning fish. When numbers get that low, a run borders on extinction. Capilano and Seymour rivers have some summer-runs, and there are some coastal rivers such as the Brem, Quatam, Little Toba and Phillips with small populations. The Coquihalla is the most accessible, and because the upper river above the canyon is fly-fishing-only, it is more appealing to anglers. Nonetheless, many anglers enjoy catching the hatchery-augmented stock in the Chehalis near Harrison Hot Springs.

Region 3 has the world-famous Thompson, and Region 5 the Chilcotin and Dean. Anglers travel from all over the world to fish the Dean, as they do celebrated waters such as the Kispiox, Bulkley, Morice, Bear, Copper, Sustut, Babine and Skeena of Region 6. There are some little-explored waters in Region 6 flowing through the Alaska Panhandle that have summer-runs, but there are none with a run on the scale of the Dean left to be discovered in the province.

Many of our summer-run steelhead waters are classified, especially those that attract attention from outside the province, such as the Thompson, Dean, Chilcotin and high-profile waters of the Skeena region.

The summer-run steelhead is a fly fisher's fish, especially during the summer and early fall months. Fly fishers will be fishing steelhead when water temperatures are in the high 40s to 60 degree F (4.5–15.5 degree C) range, optimum for fish activity. Summer-run steelhead are most active through those temperatures and will rise to take flies on or just below the surface. Whether the catch is a small 20-incher (51 cm) or a huge fish of 20 lb-plus (9 kg), summer-run steelheaders experience thrills beyond the wildest of dreams when one of those screamers grabs the fly. I get excited just writing about it.

CUTTHROAT TROUT

While the rainbow is the most abundant, largest-growing, most widely distributed trout in the province, the cutthroat is the next most abundant. Like the rainbow, the cutthroat has many colourations as a result of environment. Some sea-run cutthroat fly fishers refer to cutthroat as just "sea-runs," and "cutthroat" is often abbreviated to "cutt."

British Columbia has two types of cutthroat: Coastal and Westslope. The coastal (as the name implies) is found in Pacific coast streams and the westslope is found in streams tributary to the Columbia River and along the western slope of the Rocky Mountains. Both sub-species have the tell-tale red slash under the lower jaw, which gives the fish its common name, but on some coastal cutthroat it may be faint. Other things anglers should look for to distinguish the cutthroat from the rainbow which often frequent the same waters include tiny teeth, called hyoid teeth, on the back of the tongue, and a long upper jaw which extends well past the eye.

Furthermore, the cutthroat's body spot patterns cover more of the body, and its spots are larger than the rainbow trout's. There is quite a difference in markings between the coastal and westslope cutthroat. The coastal cutthroat has heavy spotting from head to tail and below the lateral line, while the westslope spots are more numerous on the back half of the body.

Fly fishers will find the coastal cutthroat in lakes and streams along the coastline in Regions 1, 2, 3 (Lower Fraser Canyon above Hope), 5 and 6, while the westslope cutthroat is found along the drainage flowing out of the southwestern Rocky Mountains in Regions 4, 7 and 8. Both have similar lifespans to the rainbow with maiden fish spawning in their fourth year. Like the rainbow, cutthroat are late winter and early spring spawners, and a high proportion will live to be repeat spawners.

Most waters where the cutthroat live are not as rich in food as many of the prime waters found in the Interior that rainbow enjoy. Many coastal cutthroat have adopted a migratory life cycle, journeying from river to sea in search of food. With fish growth rate directly proportional to quantity of food, and, because food sources are less abundant in cutthroat waters, it takes about five or six years to grow an 18–20-in (46–51-cm) cutthroat. As such, they are not a plentiful trout. Many sea-run populations are small and all the more fragile in the face of multiple threats to their habitat such as urbanization, logging and other resource extraction. To protect wild cutthroat stocks, the tidal waters south of Cape Caution and all mainland streams south of Jervis Inlet are catch and release on wild cutthroat. For years before it was regulated, many dedicated sea-run fly fishers practiced only catch and release and did their part to protect a loved and threatened game fish.

Although larger fish, with some over 10 lb (4.5 kg), have been taken in some of the larger coastal lakes such as Great Central, Buttle and Powell, and some isolated lakes high in the Rockies, a cutthroat of 3–4 lb (1.4–1.8 kg) taken on a fly is a trophy fish whether it be coastal or westslope.

Even though they do not grow as large, nor are they jumpers like their rainbow cousins, cutthroats will rise freely to the fly and are superb competitors, dodging, darting, occasionally jumping and twisting to shake the fly when hooked.

BROWN TROUT

When colonials first started casting their British flies on British Columbia's waters there were few fishermen and plenty of fish. As the province grew and with more fly fishers of British ancestry enjoying the sport, perhaps it was nostalgia for European fish that persuaded the government of the day to introduce the brown trout from Europe. Stockings occurred in 1932, 1933 and again in 1934 on two Vancouver Island (Region 1) streams: the Cowichan and Little Qualicum. Later, in 1957, the brown was introduced into Region 8's Kettle. More recently, browns were introduced into Somenos Lake, near Duncan.

Not many British Columbia anglers have the opportunity to fish these non-natives because they are relatively scarce, with the Cowichan having the best population. However, its population is small compared to the 3,000-brown-trout-per-mile populations that exist in famous Montana streams. Nonetheless, browns in the 5-lb (2.3-kg) range have been taken from Cameron Lake on the little Qualicum system and the Cowichan, too, has yielded a few fine specimens. The largest that guide Joe Saysell told me about was one his father caught in the distant past that tipped the scales around 11 lb (5 kg).

Because the rainbow and cutthroat may be found in the same waters as the introduced browns, anglers need to be able to tell them apart. A fall spawner sporting a brownish hue which provides its common name, the brown is a most beautifully coloured fish with large black spots, many having light or bluish haloes. This feature is quite discernible and on first sight distinguishes the brown from the cutthroat or rainbow. Any angler catching one in the 2–4-lb (0.9–1.8-kg) range has a fine specimen, although larger ones have been reported. There are some larger fish in the Cowichan, due chiefly to the mandatory catch-and-release regulations for wild browns.

Because it is a challenging fish to catch and will respond quite readily to properly selected and presented flies, the brown is a superb fly fisher's quarry.

BROOK TROUT

The brook trout or "brookie," as it is commonly called, is not a trout at all but a member of the char family. This eastern North American transplant was first introduced to British Columbia from Quebec in 1908 and is now found in all regions. It, like the transplanted brown trout, is a fall spawner. The stocking program strategy provincial fisheries adopted with the brook trout was to introduce it to barren, shallow, highly productive lakes, many of which have winter-kill problems. Brook trout do somewhat better under those conditions than do rainbow trout. Also, the lakes chosen have no streams by which the brook trout could escape into other waters, so there is no risk of cross-breeding occurring with other species.

I think anglers accept imports like the brown and the brookie quickly because they have good fighting qualities and an attractive appearance. The brook trout sports a dark green upper body, tapering to olive green along the sides with darker green vermiculations or worm-like lines on the back and dorsal fin, red spots surrounded by blue halos on the sides and pinkish-orange paired fins edged in white. Striking is certainly the word that best describes the brookie.

This fish is primarily an insect and shrimp feeder with habits similar to the rainbow. In insect-rich lakes, the brookie has rapid growth and specimens up to 9 lb (4 kg) have been taken.

I remember one trip with my son and nephew to Palmer Lake in Region 5. Palmer was slow so we went in search of other waters. On the way back to the highway we stopped at Raven Lake, located along the Palmer Lake Forest Service road. Raven, a flooded impound with many dead trees along the shore, had not quite the setting we wished, but the brookies were biting. The boys took brook trout to about 2 lb (0.9 kg) on trolled Carey Specials. Gary and

Drew Baker found some brookies on a surface feed and took fish up to 3 lb (1.4 kg) on dry flies.

Brook trout can attain weights in the 5–10-lb (2.3–4.5-kg) range. They are good fighters and excellent tasting and, with the strategy adopted by fisheries, a welcome transplant to B.C. waters.

DOLLY VARDEN AND BULL TROUT

The Dolly Varden also carries the misnomer "trout" but is really a member of the char family with a very unusual name. Like the name cutthroat, steelhead and rainbow, something about the fish's appearance produced its name, but in the dolly's case, with a twist. Dr. T. W. Lambert in *Fishing in British Columbia* (1907) recorded the name's history:

> *Its curious name is said to be derived indirectly from* [Charles] *Dickens and the time of his tours in the United States, which produced a Dolly Varden craze in hats and some kinds of calico patterns, of which one with pink spots was supposed to be the correct Dolly Varden pattern.* [Dolly Varden was a character in one of Dickens's novels.] *On seeing this fish for the first time, some young lady is supposed to have exclaimed that it was a "Dolly Varden trout," and the name appears to have been generally adopted.*

For many years the dolly's name was spoken in vain by trout fishermen, mainly because the dolly's diet consisted, besides insects and salmon eggs, of small fish, mostly trout and salmon. In days past, many fishers detested and aimlessly destroyed natural fish, animal and bird predators of trout and salmon.

B.C. anglers, with ready access to many more highly regarded game fishes, are spoiled. We judge the slower fighting qualities of the dolly too harshly against the cutthroat, rainbow, steelhead, coho and chinook. The dolly is not a runner and jumper like the trout, but a darter and tugger. It is often bad-mouthed because of those fighting qualities. However, I like to catch them, even though they are usually an incidental catch when I am fishing for steelhead, cutthroat or salmon.

Unfortunately, the dolly has a ravenous appetite. It takes most anything coming its way, is a sucker for salmon eggs and is easily susceptible to overharvest. I have pages from P. M. Smith's fishing diary for 1914, just before he went overseas to fight in World War I. He recorded for February 22 of that year a catch from the Stave River consisting of four steelhead and seven dollies to 9½ lb (94.3 kg). The total approximate weight of this catch equaled 80 lb (36 kg). Just try to find a dolly in that water now, let alone a 5–10 pounder (2.3–4.5 kg). Because they are easy to catch, dollies do not get a chance to grow large or numerous in heavily fished waters. However, more remote or protected waters often have good populations with larger fish.

For years Dolly Varden was the label of choice for this char group. Only recently have fisheries experts identified that we really have two species within the group: Dolly Varden and bull trout.

All chars spawn in the fall. Dolly Varden and bull trout are distinguished from the brook and lake trout by having no worm-like markings or vermiculations on their dorsal fin and back. They have whitish to pinkish spots on a dark background. The bull trout has a large, broad, flattened head that dominates the body, with curved upper jaw and body flattened on the underside, while the dolly has an oval, snake-like, rounder body and a small head that does not dominate the body. Both fish have white leading edges on lower fins. To the layperson, it is hard to distinguish between the two. These chars can be sea-run when present in rivers open to the ocean. When fresh in from the sea their pinkish-dotted, silvery coat is most beautiful.

Currently the distribution of dollies and bull trout is unresolved. Not long ago it was believed that the char found in coastal streams in Regions 1, 2, 3, 5 and 6 were dollies and that the bull trout was found in the rest of the province in Regions 3, 4, 5, 7 and 8. However, as identification work continues scientists are classifying more populations as bull trout, particularly in Region 2. For example, the chars found in the Squamish, Chilliwack, Coquihalla and Silverhope have been reclassified as bull trout. Occasionally dollies and bulls inhabit the same water, with the Skagit near Hope an example. In that system bull trout are found in the mainstem from Ross reservoir upstream and are large fish, whereas Dolly Varden are resident in some tributaries and are small fish.

In kokanee-rich lakes, the bull trout has attained weights of over 20 lb (9 kg), and over 10 lb (4.5 kg) in coastal streams. Fish in the 5–10-lb (2.3–4.5-kg) range are, however, good fish these days.

I researched a number of books from the turn of the last century to the present day to get this information, and most state that the dolly is not a fly fisher's fish. They are wrong. Dollies will rise to a silver-bodied fly just like the cutthroat and respond well to a deeply sunk pattern—an excellent fly fisher's quarry. I remember one day on the Lakelse so well, when the dollies just did not stop biting. The pinks were spawning and we had had good sport with cutts, whitefish and dollies the day before chucking Spratleys, egg and silver-bodied cutthroat patterns. However, with the heavy rains in the afternoon and through the night, the river was on the rise, and the next morning the fishing proved difficult. For some reason, Bob Taylor decided to try a Woolly Worm and the dollies targeted on that pattern like you would not believe. Taylor later confessed, with 30 or so dollies and trout landed, that in all his two-score-plus years on the river, he had never had a day like that with dollies. Indeed, dollies *are* a fly fisher's fish.

LAKE TROUT

Referred to by many common names, most combined with trout, this fall spawner is really a char. Originally lake trout were thought to inhabit the northern part of the province and south to Shuswap country. This char is found in Regions 3, 5, 6, 7 and 8 with limited distribution in Region 2—Alou-ette Lake only.

As the name implies, it is a fish that dwells in large, deep, often cold lakes. A fish predator, the lake trout does best in those lakes that have large numbers of fish to eat; they are common in kokanee- and sockeye-rearing lakes. Be-cause of its diet and substantial longevity it can grow large. Specimens in the 30–40-lb (13.5–18-kg) range are not uncommon. However, because it inhabits waters with a limited growing season, it may take five to 10 years to produce a large fish. A 5-pounder (2.3 kg) is a respectable size for the fly.

The lake trout resembles the bull trout. It has a long head and large snout, can have greenish, greyish or brownish colour and is heavily spotted with light-coloured, worm-like markings on the back and dorsal fin. The lake trout has a heavily forked tail.

Lake trout are not sought out by fly fishers like the other trouts and chars because it is often a deeper water fish and because it is not a vigorous fighter. Without a river current to help it, the lake trout's fight consists mainly of strong surges with plenty of head shaking and no jumps. However, they do take flies, mostly those dressed to imitate their small-fish feed, with a trolled fly most times more effective than a cast one.

KOKANEE

If you have ever caught and eaten a kokanee you will know why it is sought after by so many fishermen. The kokanee is a sockeye salmon that does not leave its freshwater environment. It is believed that they became land-locked eons ago as a result of some geological event that cut off their access to the sea. However, it is a fish that has been stocked in many waters and is now found in all regions of the province, reaching weights of 5 lb (2.3 kg) or more in some of the plankton-rich Interior lakes. In most lakes this fish does not get much larger than 2 lb (0.9 kg) with 10–12 in (25–30 cm) being common, particularly in less productive coastal lakes. In its lake environment it sports a silver coat with no distinct black spots and has the forked tail typical of all Pacific salmon. When it moves into tributaries to spawn at age three, it is an identical but smaller version of the ocean-feeding sockeye.

In years past the kokanee was not a target of sports anglers. With its natural distribution and successful plantings in many lakes, it is prolific and currently second only to the rainbow trout in numbers caught in the province. Originally the kokanee was not considered a fly fisher's fish, but that has recently changed. With its introduction into Interior fly fishing lakes rich in insects and zooplankton, kokanee in lakes such as Stump, Bridge and Horse are appearing in the 2–4-lb (0.9–1.8-kg) range. Because kokanee will take chironomids and mayflies early in the season before they go deep, they have been discovered by fly fishers.

ROCKY MOUNTAIN AND LAKE WHITEFISH

The silvery, large-scaled, herring-like, fall-spawning whitefish is not one of our more highly desired game fish, although it is one of the more plentiful fish and is found in Regions 2, 3, 4, 5, 6, 7 and 8. Fly fishers usually catch them when they are fishing for other fish, but you should know that they will take the fly, sometimes with abandon.

When trout fishing I have caught them in the Harrison, Thompson and Lakelse, to mention but a few rivers, and other anglers have told me of catches in waters they fish. To some Interior fly fishers, the whitefish is about the only fish available to satisfy that need to get out and catch something during the cold winter months.

Whitefish in streams will reach lengths of over 20 in (50 cm), with 12 in (30 cm) about average, but some streams in the South Thompson watershed have whitefish up to 4 lb (1.8 kg). Lake whitefish are found mostly in Regions 5, 6, 7, and 8 and do grow larger than their river brethren, with fish in the 3–5-lb (1.4–2.3-kg) range more common.

Bag limits at 15 fish per day are generous and an indication of high populations.

ARCTIC GRAYLING

As the name implies these fish inhabit Regions 6 and 7, the two regions in the province where waters flow north into the Arctic drainage. I am not friends with this fish as it is one of the few British Columbia game fishes that I have not caught, but I do intend to become familiar with this fish in the near future.

With its blue back, fading to purplish sides with small black spots on the front of the body and tell-tale, large purplish-spotted dorsal fin, the grayling is often referred to by those who know it as one of the most beautiful game fishes to swim North American waters.

The north country is known for its pesky insects. We may curse the bugs, but they are the main staple food of the grayling. The northern waters have a very limited growing season and it takes a number of years for grayling to become good-sized fish. Fly fishers can expect to catch grayling averaging 10–16 in (25–40 cm) in Regions 6 and 7. A 2-pounder (0.9 kg) is a very good one and larger fish, up to 4 lb (1.8 kg), come so infrequently they are considered a fish of a lifetime. The record grayling for North America came out of Great Slave Lake in the Northwest Territories. It was an ounce short of 6 lb (2.7 kg) and thought to be a whopping 13- or 14-year-old. Because of its diet and free-rising nature, the grayling is regarded as an excellent fly fisher's fish, rising to dry flies and taking wet flies with relish.

PIKE

The northern pike is another fish that is found only in the northern B.C. waters tributary to the Arctic Ocean. If you catch one, there is no mistaking the predatory pike. It is a long fish with a mottled body and razor sharp teeth. The pike attacks most things that move and can grow to a tremendous size, with fish in the 20-lb (9-kg) range in lakes not uncommon. Like the grayling, large pike in northern waters are old fish and a 10 lb (4.5 kg) pike in Region 7 waters is a good fish.

The pike has never been considered much of a fly fisher's fish and does not have the appeal of the more highly regarded species. Pike's teeth are sharp enough to sever normal fishing line, and this does not suit fly tackle. Fly anglers are seeking new challenges, and if there is a will to catch something on a fly, fly fishers will find a way. In recent years, steel leaders have become part of the pike fly fisher's arsenal and are effective against the sharp teeth. For fly fishers interested in learning more about the Arctic grayling and northern pike, I recommend Chris Hanks's *Fly Fishing in the Northwest Territories of Canada* (1996). Although mostly anecdotes on fishing the Territories, there is much information on tackle and flies mixed into the text.

SMALLMOUTH AND LARGEMOUTH BASS

Not indigenous to British Columbia, smallmouth bass have been introduced to waters in Regions 1, 4 and 8; the largemouth bass in Regions 2, 4 and 8. It is another fish that, for years after its introduction, fly fishers ignored.

However, the bass has the qualities many seek in a game fish. Although it is a game fish I have never sought, I do hear fly fishers from my own fly club talk favourably about bass in St. Mary Lake on Saltspring Island and in other Vancouver Island lakes. Region 8 has both smallmouth and largemouth bass and Okanagan fly fishers talk about the bass in Osoyoos, Vaseaux and other lakes.

Considered a regal fish in many places outside British Columbia, bass will never attain the illustrious position in British Columbia fly fishers' minds that our trout and salmon enjoy. Nonetheless, bass are a worthy game fish and many anglers enjoy the diversion.

PACIFIC SALMONS

Ever since Captain Gordon made his disparaging remarks about the Pacific Northwest having little value because the salmon would not take the fly, fly fishers have been intent on proving him wrong. And so they have. All five species of Pacific salmon are superb game fish and all can be taken on the fly, some so easily and in such numbers that you can tire of catching them.

For many years the chum, sockeye and pink were considered off limits to sport anglers and by regulation were the exclusive domain of the commercial fishing industry. The coho and chinook are two salmons that have always been fair game in rivers. Recently the federal Department of Fisheries and Oceans, which manages salmon, realized that the citizens of this province have some right to harvest these fish. With that change there has been a huge upswing in sport fishing for sockeye, pink and chums.

COHO

For over a century British Columbia fly fishers have been catching this fish on the fly in both salt and fresh water. Of all the Pacific salmons, the coho is considered the gamest of sport fish. It usually spends one year or more in fresh water before migrating to the ocean where it spends two years feeding and growing rapidly. At maturity, coho average 6–12 lb (2.7–5.4 kg), but many fish in the 15–20-lb (6.8–9-kg) class are taken in British Columbia waters every year, with the record from Cowichan Bay pushing the scale's needle to 31 lb (14 kg). All Pacific salmon are silver bright in their ocean environment. The coho's distinctive marking that sets it aside from other salmons is its white gums and its black spots speckling the back but appearing only on the upper half of the tail.

The coho is found in short to medium coastal streams and the large river systems that run well into the interior of the province in Regions 1, 2, 3, 5 and 6. For years most fly fishers sought the coho in the late summer and fall as it moved along the beaches on its spawning run, and then as it moved in from the salt water to the rivers of its birth. Some fisheries such as those of the Cowichan and Duncan bays, the Oyster River and Black Creek estuaries on Vancouver Island became well known for their coho fly fishing. However, the coho is another coastal game fish that has met hard times in recent years. Those great fisheries of yesteryear are mere fragments of their former greatness, or just mere memories.

Nonetheless, reduced runs of coho still return to streams all along the coast and there are many places that fly fishers can search with flies for the scrappy coho.

Waters such as Qualicum Bay and the estuaries of the Little and Big Qualicum rivers, the Oyster and Black Creek in Region 1 come to mind. The Harrison in Region 2 has had a fly fishery for coho since early this century. Other hatchery-augmented streams such as the Vedder and Chehalis are more confined and provide a different type of opportunity. Anglers can be elbow to elbow when the coho run is on on many hatchery rivers. Many coastal streams in Region 5 and tributaries of the Skeena in Region 6 have good coho fishing opportunities. The Queen Charlotte Islands in Region 6 probably has some of the finest coho fishing left in British Columbia.

However, coho numbers have been affected in recent years by habitat destruction, global warming and poor ocean survival. Even rivers with prolific runs have suffered. In 1997 on the Queen Charlotte Islands one of the province's most prolific coho rivers, the Tlell, was closed to coho fishing because of poor returns. Furthermore, reports during 1997 indicated that the once-majestic coho runs of the mighty Skeena are only 10 percent of the worst previous year on record. What a tragedy it will be if we lose those fisheries! We must be optimistic and hope that Nature will endure and the coho rebounds in abundance.

Shore fisheries such as those on Vancouver Island have attracted fly fishers since fly fishing for coho began. In recent years, an ocean-going breed of fly fisher has evolved who hunt the fish on the open ocean. The coho is now a fish that provides fly fishing opportunities almost all year long, from the spring blueback stage right through to when the fish move into fresh water to spawn—an April to November season.

When in the ocean and estuary the coho will rise like a trout or summer steelhead and take a fly fished just under the water's surface. Once it enters fresh water, sunk flies are more productive, but they will rise and take surface flies more readily than the other species of salmon. No matter if it takes surface or sunk flies, the coho is a very active fish when hooked. With its runs and jumps it is equal to or better than any other of the province's game fish, summer-run steelhead and rainbow trout included.

CHINOOK

The chinook is the largest of Pacific salmons, often reaching weights more than 50 lb (22.5 kg). The province's largest rod-caught chinook was a monster 92-pounder (41.4 kg) taken from the Skeena River in the 1950s. However, most fish at maturity vary between 10–50 lb (4.5–22.5 kg), and any fish over 30 lb (13.5 kg) is a good fish. Native Indians living along the coast referred to the large chinooks as Tyee, meaning chief. Sport fishers have adopted that name for any chinook 30 lb (13.5 kg) or over. Because some runs of chinook salmon start their spawning runs in the spring, it was also called a spring salmon. The chinook has the same distribution as the coho, but unlike the coho, which will run up the smallest of streams, the chinook is a big-river fish. Chinooks can be distinguished from other salmon by their black gums and black spots on both the top and bottom lobes of the tail.

Normally a deepwater fish in the ocean, it is not sought after like the coho by fly fishers. Chinook are caught, most often incidentally, by ocean coho fly fishers. However, there are a few places on the west coast of Vancouver Island and around Langara on the Queen Charlotte Islands where fly fishers are experimenting and developing successful chinook fly techniques. Nevertheless, it is when a chinook returns to its home river that it is most often taken on flies. Deep and dirty is the technique. I have taken them over 30 lb (13.5 kg) and know fishers who have battled 50-pounders (22.5 kg). Even on big rivers they can be mixed in with other salmon and will be caught incidentally. My friend Gary Baker tells a story about a young angler on the Fraser who was fly fishing for sockeye and took a chinook over 24 lb (10.8 kg). The Skeena is one of the better bets for large wild fish, but fly fishers can take chinooks if they persevere on hatchery-augmented streams such as the Kitimat, Vedder and Chehalis and all wild rivers where chinooks run.

The chinook is a strong fish that will strain the stoutest of fly tackle. Bringing chinooks to the beach is often more a matter of will: my largest—a fish of 41 in (104 cm)—ended up being a 45-minute tug-of-war before I managed to bend down and take the hook out of its jaw. You will know that you have been tested after a battle with the mighty chinook.

PINK

While the chinook is the largest Pacific salmon, the pink is the smallest. The pink averages 3–5 lb (1.4–2.3 kg) at maturity, although specimens up to 10 lb (4.5 kg) have been caught. It is found in Regions 1, 2, 3, 5 and 6 and can be distinguished from other salmons by its size. Unlike the distinct black spots that coho and chinook possess, the pink has large black splotches on the back and on the whole tail. Mature males develop a tell-tale hump and the pink's other common name, humpback, is derived from that physical attribute.

Like the chinook, the pink is an incidental catch when ocean fly fishing. However, when it returns to its stream of birth it does so in large numbers.

If the river flow is too low to attract upstream migration, pink will mill around the stream's estuary and are easily caught on flies.

The pink does not run every year to all rivers. In the south coast it runs to streams on Vancouver Island and Lower Mainland coast and Fraser River and tributaries on the odd-numbered years (1999, 2001, 2003, etc.), while on the north coast and Queen Charlotte Islands the big runs occur in even years (1998, 2000, 2002, etc.). A few streams have smaller runs every year, the Lakelse being one.

The Puntledge, Campbell, Oyster, Eve and Keogh rivers on Vancouver Island in Region 1, as well as the Fraser, Harrison and Indian rivers on the Lower Mainland's Region 2 are examples of a few streams that have good pink fisheries. In Region 6, the Skeena and its tributaries have millions of pinks in a cycle year, as do many streams on the Queen Charlotte Islands such as the Cooper, Hans, Sachs and Pallant creeks on the south island and the Tlell, Yakoun and streams in Naden Harbour on the north island.

I have spent many memorable days with my son fishing pinks, and because they are easily caught, the kids do not get bored. In the estuary, a floating line works well, but when pinks get into flowing fresh water you need to go down to them and fish a sunk fly. The pink is a head shaker with small surging runs and not a great jumper, but notwithstanding it is a fun fish to catch.

SOCKEYE

Since sport fishers on the Fraser and Skeena rivers have been allowed to take sockeye, it has become a highly sought after fish. The sockeye is not a big salmon, averaging 5–7 lb (2.3–3.2 kg) at maturity, but larger specimens up to 15 lb (7 kg) have been taken. It has a greenish blue back with fine black speckles but no spots. As they mature, the body becomes a brilliant red and the head a glorious green.

It is rare for fly fishers to take this fish in the open ocean. Most fisheries take place as the sockeye move out of the river estuary into freshwater streams. Although some rivers do have small runs of stream-reared sockeye, the abundant runs ascend rivers whose watersheds have larger lakes where sockeye fry will rear to smolt stage. Noted fisheries have developed in recent years on the Lower Fraser in Region 2 and the Skeena at Ferry Island in Region 6. However, other possibilities exist on other streams in the province, such as the Stamp and Somass in Region 1.

The fish migrate in large schools and fly fishers need to locate places in the river where large numbers are moving through. Often it requires scouring the bottom with the fly to be successful. The sockeye puts up a good scrap and is one of the best table fishes found anywhere.

CHUM

The chum is the last salmon to appear in rivers. Depending on coastal location, chum return to rivers from September through December. The chum is found in all coastal regions and is next to the sockeye and pinks in abundance. It is also the second largest salmon, after the chinook, with average weights from 8–18 lb (3.6–8.1 kg) at maturity. Many fish are over 20 lb (9 kg), with some specimens reaching 30 lb (13.5 kg). Like pink salmon, chum fry migrate to the sea almost immediately after emerging from the gravel. Once in the ocean chums will spend up to four years sea-feeding.

Like all Pacific salmon, in the ocean it has a dark, metallic-blue back with silver sides. However, because the chum is usually quite mature when it reaches the river estuary of its origin, it has already taken on tell-tale longitudinal splotches, usually of a dusky red or purplish colour. As they mature, the males grow large canine-like teeth and for that reason are commonly called dog salmon.

The chum probably takes the fly more violently than any other salmon and is an extremely powerful opponent, running out much line and often jumping when hooked.

Many rivers and small streams have runs of chums, but despite this it is not as widely fished as returning coho because it usually returns later in the fall. Fly fishers journeying to places like Qualicum Bay on Vancouver Island and the Harrison and many other chum streams throughout the province will tell tales about this hard-fighting fish. Make sure you have strong tackle: chums will put whatever tackle you use to the supreme test.

Variety is said to be the spice of life, and with about a dozen and a half game fish that range from a few ounces to over 50 lb (22.5 kg), the game fishes of British Columbia offer much spice for the fly fisher. With so many game fishes to consider, fly fishers need be able to present their flies in a variety of ways using proper equipment. That is the focus of the next chapter.

CHAPTER THREE

Fly Fishing Options

Blessed with many game fish to challenge in lake, stream and sea, British Columbia fly fishers will need to make basic decisions about which fish or fishes to angle for with what tackle, flies and other ancillary equipment. Once you have the basic gear, you need to get out and do some fishing, because fly fishing knowledge is a cumulative thing. Each experience builds on the previous ones, and as years go by and you become old and grey or bald like me there is not as much second-guessing on what to use and how to present it. The fish come much easier. Through the early years you need to endure the impatience of youth and, as with any worthwhile endeavour, realize that the path to becoming a master takes time and effort. Over the past three decades, I have seen many places and caught many fish. I cannot think of a more enjoyable thing to do than spend a lifetime learning about fish and fly fishing. The places you get to, the people you meet and the fish you catch are but a few of the rewards.

However, for some fly fishers recreational time is precious and little can be devoted in a year to the contemplative man's recreation. Doctors are a group that especially comes to mind in that regard, but there are many others. For those, a guided trip may be the answer. Not all guides cater only to fly fishers;

many are generalists who may not be expert fly fishers. Nevertheless, making a living from only fly fishing guiding is difficult, and generalists might be the only guides available in some parts of the province. When my son was young and we wanted to go to the Queen Charlotte Islands for a spring break vacation, I had a generalist guide friend whom I hired. I fly fished while the guide helped my boy float fish. We both caught fish and had a good time. Nonetheless, even if you decide a guide is for you, the more you know about how to catch your quarry, the better off you are.

British Columbia has many good fly fishing guides—some world renowned. Some are independents, while others work for lodge owners where guide services are part of a fly fishing package. Some fly fishing shops often act as booking agents for lodges besides being able to direct you to independent guides in their area. For example, in the Lower Mainland where I live, fishing shops such as Ruddick's, Michael & Young, Hanson's Fishing Outfitters and Babcock's Fly & Tackle either act as agents, can direct you to independent guides or have guides working as sales representatives. Tyson Gogel of Ruddick's and Kelly Davison of Babcock's are a couple of Region 2 guides working as sales representatives who hire out by the day. Kelly Davison's specialty is fly fishing the Lower Fraser River and tributaries for steelhead, cutthroat and salmon. Tyson Gogel, in his days off from Ruddick's, works as an assistant guide to Neil McCutcheon of Brackendale, near Whistler, and guides clients for trout, salmon and steelhead. Most fly fishing shops can recommend guides working in their area who are knowledgeable and keen. In addition, many destination fishing lodges and resorts belong to the British Columbia Fishing Resort and Outfitters Association, and many association members have guides available on a permanent or casual basis. Each year the association publishes a magazine about freshwater fishing opportunities with a list of members and contacts.

Freshwater guiding is regulated by the provincial government, with each region licensing and administering Angling Guides and Assistant Angling Guides doing business in their region. Furthermore, unless a person is licensed by the province to guide on specific waters, it is illegal for an individual to charge a fee to take someone fishing, recognized fishing schools exempted. There are individuals from in-province and out-of-province who organize trips, charge fees and accompany the group who are conducting illegal guiding operations. In some Canadian provinces non-residents cannot fish unless they are accompanied by a licensed guide, and perhaps that may be the solution adopted here. I hope not, but the few greedy fishing professionals may spoil it for all.

Regional fisheries offices can provide information about who guides on what waters, but staff cannot make recommendations. When seeking guide service, whether it be from an independent or through a lodge or resort, you need to tell them that you are a fly fisher and specify the target fish and the type of fishing—lake, river or ocean—that you desire. If river fishing is your pleasure but you have difficulties in getting about on shore, then you need to ask about transportation.

Earlier this year I had a call from a German fly fisher who wanted so much to catch a steelhead using the skated or dry fly techniques. The gentleman was a school teacher and his trip to North America—a many-thousand-dollar expense—would probably be a once-in-a-lifetime experience. Complicating his desire to catch a steelhead on the fly was his confinement to a wheelchair. That meant he probably needed a guide and I gave a couple of names who might be able to help him, although I was doubtful. Not only would this fly fisher need a guide, but also he would need to be allowed to fly fish from a boat. That further restricted his options because so many summer-run steelhead rivers do not permit angling from boats. Here was a fly fisher who knew what he wanted to do, how and when he wanted to do it, but because of a physical limitation his options were few and the cost probably beyond his means. Eventually, I suggested he contact the Canadian Paraplegic Association to see if they might be able to help him.

Nonetheless, for many, British Columbia's professional guides with their experience and knowledge can bridge that time-to-gain-experience gap. They know their waters, they know the fish and, in many cases, they can get you into less crowded places whether they be on the sea after salmon, on rivers after salmon, steelhead and trout, or on lakes for the famous rainbow. Guides are often a worthwhile investment to the fly fisher with limited recreational time or for those wanting to explore new waters in some of the more distant waters of the province.

Before we get into details on tackle and flies, a few words are appropriate about fly fishing outfits and hooks. In the 1960s the American Fishing Tackle Association (AFTA) devised a numbering system for fly-fishing equipment which matched lines to rods. The smaller the number, the more delicate the outfit, with numbers 3 to 5 suitable for smaller fish in lake and stream, 6 to 8 suitable for medium-sized fish (or even small fish if you must punch a line through a stiff wind) and 9 to 11 for larger fish such as steelhead and salmon.

Hooks on which flies are dressed are designated by a numbering system that ranges from 1 to 28, where 1 is large and 28 is tiny. Hooks larger than 1 are designated by a /o after the number (e.g., 1/o, 2/o, etc.). Trout flies are usually dressed on hooks from about 6 to 14, and steelhead and salmon flies are dressed on hooks from about 8 to 3/o.

STILLWATER TACKLE AND FLIES

A 2-lb fish on most British Columbia lakes is a prize and can be handled easily with a #4 or #5 fly-fishing outfit, but you never know when a fish of 5–10 lb (2.3–4.5 kg) will grab your fly. When that happens, you owe it to the fish to get it in quickly and not play it to death, so a #6 or #7 outfit is perhaps a better choice for all-round lake fishing. Even a #8 is in order if you want a multi-use rod for trout, beach salmon fishing and summer-run steelhead fly fishing. I use a #5, 8'6" (2.6 m) Hardy bamboo rod that I prefer for my trout fishing, but I also pack a #7 graphite rod just in case I have to punch a line through a stiff breeze or I decide to do some trolling.

For stillwaters, you should have three lines: a floater and medium and fast sinkers. The floater is for presenting floating flies, subsurface wet flies and nymphs in shallow water along reed beds and over shoals, and for presenting chironomids and bloodworms. The medium sinker is required for fishing all types of wet flies nearer the bottom, and a faster sinker is needed for trolling.

Many lake fly fishers frown on trolling, but it sure helps you get to know a lake. Often, during tough fishing times such as the summer doldrums, trolling can be the only effective way of catching trout.

There are hundreds of fly patterns appropriate to British Columbia waters, with each local area having its favourites. There are certain fauna that live in lakes, and the angler needs to have a selection of flies that could be representative of the size and shape of small fish such as salmon fry or sticklebacks, leeches, shrimp, chironomids, bloodworms, mayflies, sedges, damselfly and dragonfly nymphs and water boatmen. Some flies require a creative imagination to marry the fly with any particular bug or small fish. They are just such good fish catchers we use them despite their lack of resemblance to anything in nature.

What fly to choose and where to start are questions that plague the beginner fly fisher planning a trip in British Columbia. With a little thought and prudent purchases of some choice patterns, the novice, whether new to fly fishing or just new to the province, can have a better chance at success.

Confidence in a fly pattern is paramount to success. If you do not have confidence in what you are using you tend to flit from pattern to pattern and do not concentrate the effort into the fishing that you do if you know that the fly on the end of the line catches fish.

Confidence in a fly comes from success, which for the beginner or visiting angler can take time. Someone new to the sport or province must value and trust the knowledge and advice of those more experienced. Sound advice and well-tied patterns purchased from a reputable fly shop are a couple of basics that will start you on the right track.

Confidence with a particular pattern builds as the fish come to the fly. Eventually you develop the utmost—but never let it get to be blind—faith in the pattern. You still must be observant of insect hatches, taking into account the weather and water conditions and vary the size and pattern to suit those observations. As a rule, you do not tie on a #2 fly when fish are feeding on insects represented in size by a #12. I say as a rule, but sometimes it is worth a try if all your offerings are for naught. A drastic change can sometimes produce a reaction from a fish. Nothing in fly fishing is absolute.

The following patterns have lengthy histories with admirable records and broad use in the province. Some are multi-purpose, and most should be available at fly fishing shops throughout the province.

Carey Special: A staple pattern in many anglers' fly boxes is the Carey Special. Its origins date back to the 1920s when Colonel Carey, a retired British soldier, moved from Victoria to the Okanagan and sought to develop patterns that would catch fish in the Beaver Lake chain near Kelowna.

Now it is used all over the province and elsewhere in sizes #2 to #12. According to Tommy Brayshaw who met the Colonel at Lac Le Jeune in 1934, the fly's original dressing consisted of a tail, body and wing of marmot (groundhog) hair. The fly is now dressed with many body variations and is one of British Columbia's most productive patterns.

According to Steve Raymond in his book, *Kamloops* (1971), the Carey Special, tied on a #6 hook, was intended to represent a hatching sedge pupa, but some claim that later, as the dressings became sparser and other body colours became popular, the medium-sized Carey Special came to represent a damselfly nymph, and the larger, fuller-winged Careys a dragonfly nymph. For whatever reason the fish take the fly, it is a very successful pattern and can be effective either cast and retrieved, or trolled.

As a trolled fly, it is an excellent pattern for searching a lake. Put a #4 or #6 Carey Special on a sinking line and scout the perimeter of the lake, trying to follow the drop-off contour. Using Polaroid glasses I like to be able to see bottom on one side of the boat and deep water on the other. With a Carey Special on my fly line, with just about all the line out, I am confident of success if the fish are there.

The dressing I prefer is:

Hook: #6 or #4 Mustad 9672

Tail: A few fibres from a ring-neck cock pheasant rump feather

Body: Dark-olive seal fur or wool

Wing: Ring-neck cock pheasant rump feather wound as a collar, fairly sparse

Other popular body colours are green, yellow, red and black. I dress an all-black Carey variation with a body of black mohair and black-dyed pheasant rump collar and use it as a leech imitation.

Doc Spratley: This is a favourite of many stilllwater fly fishers, but it has a wide following with river fishers as well. I have so many fond memories associated with the pattern that when I am not sure what to use the Doc Spratley often ends up on my line. I rarely regret that decision. I have the utmost confidence in this fly's ability to attract fish. Developed in the late 1940s and popularized in the interior lakes of British Columbia by Dr. Donald Spratley, a Mt. Vernon, Washington, dentist, this is such a consistent fish catcher it is a quick confidence builder.

Originally, this fly was tied on a #6 hook. Now it is dressed in sizes from #14 to #2. The smaller Spratleys should be sparser and have bodies of floss or wool, while the larger may be dressed more fully with chenille.

The Doc Spratley in its larger sizes is similar in size to some dragonfly nymphs and in size and shape to some minnows, one of the reasons it is excellent trolled—equal to if not better than the Carey Special. The same techniques used for trolling the Carey apply to the Spratley. In its smaller sizes, say #14 to #8, particularly if tied sparsely, it is the same size and representative of a chironomid pupa and is then better cast and retrieved. As a chironomid imitation, the slower the retrieve the better. To make it appear more representative when fishing it as a chironomid pupa, some anglers clip the wing off just behind the head.

The dressing is:

Hook: #12 to #2 Mustad 9672
Tail: Guinea fowl fibres
Body: Black floss, wool or chenille
Rib: Silver tinsel
Throat: Guinea fowl
Wing: Strips of ring-neck pheasant tail feather
Head: Peacock herl

The Doc Spratley dressed with a red, green, olive or brown body has proven effective in certain locations, but none can match the fish-catching consistency of the original black-bodied fly.

Tom Thumb: In the early days of fly fishing in the province it was not uncommon for fish of 10 lb (4.5 kg) or so to be taken on dry flies. There is only one insect that brings large fish up to the surface, and only some of the Interior lakes have them. That is the "travelling sedge." These medium-to-large caddisflies pop to the surface when hatching and scamper over the surface causing quite a disturbance. The fish find them irresistible. Every fisherman should have something in his arsenal just in case he finds himself on a lake when the sedges are coming off. The Tom Thumb is the choice of many.

According to Martin Tolley, the founding president of British Columbia's first fly-fishing club, the Totem Fly Fishers, the Tom Thumb made its debut in Jasper, Alberta. The late Collie Peacock, long-time guide, tackle store operator and salesman, is credited with popularizing it in British Columbia and providing its name. Collie recalled meeting a California dentist who was using the fly in Jasper, but Collie could recall neither the origin of the fly, its name nor that of the dentist fishing it, so he pulled the name "Tom Thumb" out of his hat. No other dry fly has the fame of or is more widely used in British Columbia than the Tom Thumb.

The fly is constructed totally of deer hair and is almost unsinkable. An ample supply of flies is needed though, because deer hair is not durable and the trout's teeth do rip these flies apart.

The dressing is:

Hook: #8 to #14 Mustad 94840
Tail: Deer hair
Body: Deer hair
Hackle: Deer hair

This fly, besides being a good sedge imitation, if dressed sparsely also can double as a mayfly imitation and is effective when fished wet, either cast and retrieved or trolled. Besides lakes, the Tom Thumb is an excellent dry fly for river fly fishing, with larger patterns being effective for steelhead.

Halfback: The Halfback, developed in the late 1950s and the brainchild of John Dexheimer of Savona, is an excellent multi-purpose pattern. In its smaller sizes, trout take it for a chironomid pupa or the nymphal stage of the *Callibaetis* mayfly. In larger sizes it resembles a shrimp, and even larger a damselfly or dragonfly nymph. As a cast fly, using various retrieves, it has been catching fish consistently in British Columbia since its introduction.

In May 1991, Bob Taylor and I found ourselves on Leighton Lake, near Logan Lake Village. The spring had been exceptionally wet and, in general, the Interior lake fishing poor. The conditions we experienced were not unusual for the season, but sometimes May fishing can be really hot. This May it was not, but we persisted, and rowed around the lake casting into likely spots, hoping for a fly hatch to put the fish into a taking mood. No hatch developed, nor did the fish get into a taking mood, but we managed to attract a couple of fish. Later in the day we came across an area where there were numerous fish showing, but sometimes fish just jump and do not take well. Nevertheless we persevered, trying various patterns and sizes of fly. Every now and then we would hook a fish on a Carey or Spratley. Eventually, Bob put on a Halfback and it appealed more to the finny creatures below. We fished until day's end and the next morning before we headed home, and our catch was impressive compared with others. One regular visitor to the lake, who had put in a good day, had nothing to show for his effort. He came over later, wanting to know what our magic fly was. Although he had numerous Halfbacks in his box, he had neglected to try them. We went home happy. The Halfback nymph had saved our trip.

Originally, the Halfback was dressed on a #6, 2x long hook, but nowadays it is dressed in many sizes. Those dressed on #8 and #10 hooks are good general sizes to have. Sometimes a little lead is wrapped on the shank under the dressing. The lead helps sink the fly to a feeding depth more quickly.

The dressing is:

Hook: #6 to #12 Mustad 9672
Body: Bronze peacock herl with a wing case of ring-neck pheasant
Rib: Fine silver wire
Throat: Brown hackle

A variant of the Halfback pattern called the Fullback (also developed by John Dexheimer), tied with a wing case extending the length of the body, is also an effective fly.

Werner Shrimp: Roderick Haig-Brown, in his book *The Western Angler* (1939) was among the first British Columbia fly fishermen to note the importance of the freshwater shrimp, *gammarus,* as a trout food and, therefore, the need for the fly fisher to try effective imitations. Haig-Brown found that his gammarus imitation caught fish just about everywhere in the province that he tried it, but he also commented that his pattern was probably not as good as what might be produced.

Much later, sometime in the 1960s, the Werner Shrimp, a gammarus imitation developed by professional fly-dresser Mary Stewart and popularized by Werner Schmid, both of Vancouver, became a popular pattern. Originally, the fly was tied on #6 or #8 hooks, which are larger than most shrimps. Now the pattern is dressed on smaller hooks closer in size to the actual crustacean.

The dressing is:

Hook: #12 to #8 Mustad 3906 or 3906 B
Tail: Deer hair
Body: Olive seal fur or chenille
Hackle: Brown, palmered
Back: Deer hair

A more faithful gammarus imitation is dressed with grey or olive-green seal fur and a shell back of clear plastic, bound with fine gold or silver wire, and finished with a corresponding grey or olive throat.

Chironomid Pupa: Most serious fly fishers in this province know that chironomids are a valuable source of food early in the season for trout, and that black-bodied imitations of them seem the most productive. However, chironomid pupae are also found in shades of brown, green, orange and red. In May 1994, I spent a few days on Hihium Lake and managed to do okay using a dark-olive-bodied fly. However, with a catch to prove it, two Vancouver enthusiasts camped next to me expounded the virtues of a green-bodied Spratley. Later, as that evening drew to a close, I kept a fish of about 1½ lb (0.7 kg) for the pot and when I cleaned it I noticed a large bulge in the stomach. Although the mass of food had some other light coloured "bloodworms" or chironomid larvae and some darker pupae, the mass was a bright green. There are times when fish will target size, shape or colour and in this case I believe that the two Vancouver fly fishers' success can be attributed to their use of a fly of the fishes' targeted colour.

Black chironomid pupa imitations are usually more productive because they are more common. The dressing for a black-bodied pattern is:

Hook: #10 to #16, 4 extra long
Body: Black floss tapered to front of hook
Rib: Fine silver tinsel
Thorax: Grouse feather
Gills: White acrylic yarn
Legs: Grouse feather fibres

Another popular favourite is Brian Chan's Red-butted Chironomid. The dressing is:

Hook: #10 to #16
Tag: Bright red floss or yarn
Body: Dark brown pheasant tail fibres
Rib: Flat gold tinsel
Thorax: Peacock herl with pheasant tail shellback
Gills: White acrylic yarn or ostrich

Leeches: Trout are always on the lookout for food. Leeches are one of the larger food items in a lake and a mouthful for hungry fish. You should not travel to any lake in the province without a leech pattern. A good leech pattern will take fish even on those lakes that do not have leeches. One of the more effective and popular leech patterns, developed by Jack Shaw of Kamloops, is the Blood Leech:

Hook: #6 or #8 Mustad 9672
Tail: Brushed-out blended maroon and black wool or seal fur
Body: Same as tail

There are many other leech imitations, and the ever-popular black, dark brown and olive Woolly Buggers are effective substitutes for locally recommended imitations.

The experienced fly fisher planning a trip to British Columbia or someone just learning can use the above selection as a guide, assured that he or she will have a good start with flies that were developed for British Columbia's stillwaters and will work well. Because of personal experience or knowledge, you may be persuaded to switch to other patterns.

Nonetheless, a word of caution: know the fish that you are pursuing, and until you gain experience, you must avoid the "change-fly syndrome" of having so many patterns in your box that you are constantly searching for the "right one," never giving any fly a real chance.

Be observant of other anglers. Watch for consistent fish-catchers. Study their techniques and where they are fishing. Observe natural conditions; wind plays a factor in where and how to fish. Fish are hard to catch during bright, hot, sunny days when the lake, river or sea surface is glassy. A rippling breeze can disturb the water surface enough to make fish more easily lured. Fish feeding activity is important. If you observe an insect hatch come on putting fish "on the take" at 10 a.m. one day, chances are if the weather and water conditions remain the same the hatch will happen the next day at the same time. If there are successful anglers nearby, try to find out what they are using. You may not have the same fly, but try to match the size, shape and colour of their fly with one of the basic patterns you do have. The next day, be there and be ready, before the previous day's activity time. Often these prime taking times will prove of short duration—Nature does not wait. Combining these strategies with a few proven, established flies in various sizes, and concentrating your efforts on fishing these basic patterns with conviction and faith will improve your chances considerably.

A good starting selection would include the following patterns and sizes: #6 Carey Special; #4, #8 and #12 Doc Spratley; #8 and #12 Tom Thumb; #8 and #12 Halfback; #8 and #12 Werner Shrimp; #10, #12 and #14 Chironomids, and #6 Blood Leech.

Throw in some Woolly Buggers and Muddlers and you have ample choice. As you gain knowledge and experience, you can add other patterns.

STILLWATER TECHNIQUES

Generally, other than the small amount of time when some insects migrate to the surface to hatch, most insects and crustacea spend the majority of their lives close to the bottom, in water less than 30 ft (9 m) deep. Most flies need to be fished as close to the bottom as practical without hanging up. There are various presentation techniques that marry with the flies you intend to use and with systematic exploration of a lake.

Although there may be places on many lakes where a fly fisher could cast from shore and catch some fish, most stillwaters are best fished from a boat, float tube or pontoon floating device. Visitors coming to the province, if they are not staying at a lodge or resort where a boat is supplied or rentals available, will need to bring a watercraft. The popular one-person belly or tube boats are quite suitable for smaller lakes. Indeed, some fly fishers would say they are the only way to fish and belly boats in particular are easily packed into hike-in lakes, providing the fly fisher with more choice. However, if you have to travel a considerable distance on the lake to the fishing grounds, a boat with a motor is a must.

If your destination stillwater is new to you, trolling a fly is an excellent way of working the lake and learning more about it. Whether you are fishing from a belly boat, pontoon or conventional boat, stick on a sinking line with a Carey Special, Doc Spratley or other favourite—Woolly Buggers are well known throughout North America and are excellent for this type of exploration—and work the edges of the drop-off. Observe other anglers and particularly those catching fish.

The troll-and-cast technique complements searching for fish and can be very effective with two anglers fishing from a boat, preferably a rowed or wind-propelled boat. One partner maintains a course while trailing his line off the stern while the other fisher casts his fly at right angles towards shore or over a shoal. Fresh in my mind is a trip into Region 8 with my son to fish Kump Lake.

We hit the end of a good stretch of weather, and with deteriorating fishing conditions, we used the troll-and-cast technique. While I rowed my son cast his sedge pattern into the shallows and outfished my trolled fly 10:1. He landed about 40 to 50 trout with a couple of 16-inchers (41 cm) over the three days and caught more fish than any other fly fisher in our group, most of whom were fishing solo and using other techniques.

Sunk-line, dry fly and chironomid are three techniques that suit fishing from a motionless boat. Remember, most fish feed near the bottom and successful fly fishers fish down to them. With a sinking line and a shrimp, Spratley, leech or other suitable pattern, the fly fisher casts the line and lets it sink into the fish's travelling and feeding zone, usually, as I said, near the bottom. The idea is to fish a fly a couple of feet or so (0.5 m) above and parallel to the bottom using a hand-twist or short, stripping-of-the-line-type retrieve. Fast sinking high-density lines sink quickly, but slower intermediate or sink-tip lines are more suitable to this technique. Sink-tip lines are easier to use. While a full-sink intermediate will take a little longer to sink it does offer better control of fly-fishing depth and superior presentation and, in the minds of many experienced stillwater fishers, is the right tool for this technique.

Depending on the depth of water, you will need to keep track of the amount of time between the cast and the start of the retrieve. If you get hung up on bottom when you start or shortly after you begin the retrieve, you have let the line sink too deep. If you start catching fish right away, however, you are fishing the correct depth and should work that zone, only varying the depth when the fish stop biting.

Later in this text I discuss comprehensively chironomid fly-fishing techniques using a floating line; however, a full sinker can be used to fish a chironomid off the stern of the boat. Using as an example 15 ft (4.5 m) of water depth, cast 14 ft (4.2 m) of line including leader, let it sink vertically, then slowly twitch it up the water column. With such a short line and little cushion, be prepared for violent strikes and the odd broken leader.

A floating line combined with a chironomid, wet fly or dry fly can be used effectively to fish for feeding fish, from those taking insects hatching on the surface to those feeding on bloodworms or chironomids in about 20 ft (6 m) of water.

Seeing a fish come to the surface and take a fly is one of the true thrills of fly fishing. In British Columbia stillwater fisheries there are two insects available for surface-feeding trout that predominate over others: the sedge or caddisfly and the mayfly. Not all stillwaters have either insect, and few have both. Those that do can provide some thrilling moments.

A floating line with a green- or grey-bodied sedge pattern or the good old reliable Tom Thumb is all that is needed. Place your boat over a shoal with hatching sedges or mayflies and cast a dry fly toward a seen fish or, if a fish is in a travel pattern, a little ahead of the fish. Leave a mayfly imitation still, but you can skitter a sedge imitation over the surface. Once a sedge pops to the surface, it often scampers across the water causing quite a commotion, which often attracts the attention of bottom-cruising fish. Sometimes it is worthwhile to draw some line, skating the fly and mimicking the real thing.

I remember one trip Gary Baker and I took with our boys to Jacques Lake in Region 5. I had to leave early and decided to row around the forestry campsite end of the lake, while Gary ventured a considerable distance to the far end of the lake. With the sedges popping and the fish taking them with abandon, Gary and Drew had wonderful fishing with fish up to 5 lb (2.3 kg) on the dry fly. To this day Gary likes to remind me of what I missed.

Often the floating line teamed with a shrimp, Spratley or leech is a good combination to fish shallow water over shoals and along reed beds. Using a full sinker or sink tip would create too many bottom hang-ups.

Chironomids, or midges as they are know elsewhere, are a very abundant and important food source in many of our stillwater fisheries. Trout feed on chironomid larvae (commonly called bloodworms because of their often-red hemoglobin colour) on the bottom. They take the pupae near the bottom and all the way up the water column when they are hatching, and, when hatching, the adult in the surface film. However, it is the pupal form that most fishers imitate. A chironomid pupa imitation with a floating line is a good combination for fishing chironomids in water up to and sometimes greater than 20 ft

(6 m) deep. To fish chironomids effectively requires a still boat, and double an-choring is recommended. The depth the fly will be fishing needs to be mea-sured with a sounding line—often anglers mark an anchor line—and the leader adjusted so that the pupa imitation fishes about 1 ft (0.3 m) above the bottom, in the travel zone of fish searching for food. Some anglers inch the pu-pae to the boat while others attach a strike indicator and mooch the fly, strik-ing when the indicator moves or is towed under by a taking fish.

Chironomid imitations lack mass and take a considerable time to sink to a depth of 10 ft (3 m) or more. Many fly fishers dress their imitations with lead underbodies to provide more mass and help sink the fly quicker. Others attach a small split shot ahead of the fly on the leader. However, on fly-fishing-only waters external weighting of the leader or floating of the line with an attached float is outside the limits of what is allowed. Check the regulations to be sure if you are fishing waters designated for only flyfishing or artificial flies. (Fly-fishing-only and artifical-flies definitions are included in Appendix B.)

RIVER AND STREAM TACKLE AND FLIES

In river and stream fishing, the range in fish size can be extreme. Many anglers have outfits ranging from #4 to #11 to cover this diversity. For example, when I fish trout streams I know that a 4 lb (1.8 kg) trout is a good one and for me easily handled with a #5 outfit. On many of our steelhead rivers the average fish may be 8–10 lb (3.6–4.5 kg), but most streams will have some fish in the 15–20-lb (7–9-kg) range with the occasional one even larger. In some rivers such as the Thompson and Kispiox, fish between 15–20 lb (7–9 kg) are com-mon and over 20 lb (9 kg) frequent. To satisfy my steelhead fly-fishing require-ments I generally use outfits in the #8 to #11 range. If the lordly chinook is about, a #9 outfit is about the minimum you would need to tackle those beasts. For the smaller pink salmon a #5 to #7 outfit is quite adequate.

I prefer river fishing to any other. Because of that preference I use special equipment and own three double-handed Spey rods of 12, 15 and 17½ ft (3.6, 4.5 and 5.3 m) that throw lines varying from #8 to #11. If you do lake fishing and have a #7 outfit and are going to do a fair amount of river fishing for fish greater than 10 lb (4.5 kg), you could cover most large-fish river fishing with a #9 outfit with the #7 stillwater outfit being your back-up.

There is a huge variety of lines suitable for river fishing—ranging from full floaters, floaters with sink tips to full sinkers. A floating line is a must for presenting flies near or on the surface and for nymph fishing. Being a steelhead specialist I prefer to Spey cast even with a single-handed rod and use a double-taper floating line over the now popular weight forward. Nonetheless, the weight-forward lines are well designed, cast well and are preferred by many.

Most fish in rivers are bottom dwellers, and although some can be taken on flies on or near the surface, much of the time you must fish down to them. To accomplish this task, a fly fisher should have at least a couple of lines that sink: a fast sinker for slower moving water and a super-fast sinker for deeper and/or faster moving water. Most fly fishers have abandoned the full sinkers for river fishing and go with sink tips. I make my own sink tips and have extra-fast to slow sink tips, ranging from 5–16 ft (1.5–4.8 kg) in length, which I loop onto my double-taper #9, #10 or #11 floater for steelhead fly fishing. I do own numerous manufactured sink tips for salmon and trout fly fishing. For steelhead and salmon fishing you must at times dredge the bottom. Many fly fishers use one of the "Teeney T" series of tips for their extra-fast tip, while others prefer a couple of sink tips from Cortland's or Scientific Anglers' series of lines. Big fish in flowing water usually require a larger-capacity reel and 100–200 yd (90–180 m) of backing, depending on size of river and fish. Big chinooks and steelhead on large rivers can take much line.

Fishing with a floating line requires a transfer of energy through the fly line and leader to the fly. A tapered leader helps transfer the energy and present the fly properly. However, you do not need costly tapered leaders for sunk-line fishing. For sunk-line, you attach directly to the end of your sink-tip or full-sinking line a 3–4-ft (0.9–1.2-m) section of tippet material of the test that is needed to match the type of fish angled for: about 5 lb (2.3 kg) tippet for trout, 10 lb (4.5 kg) for small salmon and summer-run steelhead and 12–15 lb (5.4–6.8 kg) for large steelhead and salmon.

The purpose of fishing a sunk line is to get the fly down to proper fishing depth quickly. On fast-flowing rivers, if you use a 9–12-ft (2.7–3.6-m) tapered leader, often your drift is complete by the time the fly has had a chance to sink very deep. By using a short leader attached directly to the fly line, the fly will sink with the line and be down to maximum fishing depth promptly, resulting in a better drift and presentation. Some fly fishers dress their flies with lead and others attach a small split shot to make sure the fly sinks quickly.

There are hundreds of flies that could be used for fly fishing in this province's rivers and streams. However, fish are often curious creatures. They are predators and, unlike humans who pick things up with their hands for examination, fish have only their mouths to test things. That is often our goal: put something tempting enough and close enough to the fish that it takes it into its mouth. The problem of fly selection becomes more confounding when you consider the numbers of fish that can be angled for in the rivers and streams. However, the selection process can be simplified somewhat if you segregate between feeding and non-feeding fish.

Trout that live their entire lives in fresh water need to feed to grow big. Other fish such as the steelhead and Pacific salmon go to the sea and grow large, then return as non-feeders during the spawning run. Some flies appeal to feeders, some to non-feeders, and some work well for both. I hope to simplify selection by providing a limited list of flies that can be used in most rivers and for a variety of fish. Not all anglers will agree with my choices, and that is fine. For example, I know from experience that I can use a certain fly on any given steelhead stream and, as long as the water temperature, clarity, river velocity and light conditions are similar, I will catch fish.

In the following list of flies for river fishing, I have tried to include some flies that are used for stillwaters to limit overall gear requirements. The selection is not exhaustive, but it will get you started.

The Doc Spratley, with the dressing given in the stillwater section and in the smaller sizes, is a good trout fly in some rivers. It is popular as a floating-line fly for summer-run steelhead when dressed on #6–#1/0 low-water salmon hooks.

Two other flies mentioned in the stillwater section that are also good river

trout flies are the Halfback and Tom Thumb. The Halfback in its many variations is representative of mayfly and smaller stonefly nymphs often found in
river environments. The Tom Thumb is a good floater and will take fish on just
about any stream in the province if they are rising to dries. With so many
salmon-bearing streams throughout the province and the salmon fry emergence in the spring a feast for resident trout, silver-bodied fry patterns such as
Mallard & Silver, Egg 'n' I, Tinsel and Bucktail are a must.

The details for dressing these flies are:

Mallard & Silver

Hook: #2–#8 low-water salmon

Body: Flat silver tinsel

Wing: Strips of grey mallard breast feather

The Egg 'n' I is a Mallard & Silver with a tuft of fluorescent red wool tied
in at the throat. It is representative of an alevin (new-hatched salmon) just out
of gravel and still bearing remnants of its yolk sac.

The Tinsel is similar to the Mallard & Silver but has a darker wing of
strips from the male hooded merganser. A bronze mallard wing is a good substitute for the merganser.

Bucktail

Hook: #2/o–#8

Body: Flat silver tinsel

Wing: Brown, red and white, blue and white, or green and white hair
            from a deer's tail, often with a few strands of Krystal flash (The
            Bucktail is more effective when dressed with polar bear hair,
            which is more translucent and radiant than deer tail.)

Rolled Muddler: The stickleback is a small baitfish found in most waters and
is an important source of food in many lakes, streams and estuaries. Tom Murray's Rolled Muddler is one of the better imitations and is used throughout
the province. The dressing is:

Hook: #8–#12, Mustad 9671 (2x long)

Tail: Light mallard

Body: Silver mylar

Rib: Oval tinsel, wound reverse to mylar

Wing: Rolled or slender strips of light mallard flank feather

Head: Deer hair, spun and clipped with a few strands of deer hair extending down along the body (Use red tying thread and tie deer hair in so that there is some red thread showing behind and in front of the head.)

A Muddler Minnow dressed in the same sizes is a reasonable substitute for Murray's fly. Larger Muddlers are effective on some trout and steelhead streams.

Black Caterpillar: One of my favourites for trout river fishing and a fly that can be used for steelhead is Roderick Haig-Brown's Black Caterpillar. Haig-Brown found this fly effective when the carpenter ant hatch was on, and I have found it effective as a good search pattern on a number of waters that I fish. The dressing is:

Hook: #6 or #8 for trout and up to #2 for steelhead

Body: Black seal fur

Rib: Fine, oval gold with a strand of bronze peacock herl

Hackle: Black

The ever-popular Woolly Worm, dressed with a black chenille body and palmered grizzly hackle, is another all-purpose pattern. Anglers may want to substitute it for the Black Caterpillar if they are not fly tyers.

Include some partridge-hackled flies such as Partridge and Hares Ear, Partridge and Orange, Partridge and Peacock, Hares Ear nymph and perhaps an Adams dry fly in sizes #14, #12 and #10 as well as a #6 stonefly nymph, and you will have a basic selection that will cover most stream trout fishing situations.

There are hundreds of steelhead patterns from which a fly fisher can choose and each locale will have its favourites. Over many years fishing many rivers, I have surmised that an experienced fly fisher using sound judgement needs only five basic patterns, if the fisher is able to marry size and pattern to water and light conditions and presentation techniques.

The five basic patterns are: a large fly such as the General Practitioner for coloured and or cold water conditions, for use in poor light and more often for use on a sunk line; a short-bodied, quick-sinking pattern such as the Cowichan Coachman for use in nymph-type presentations; a slim-bodied pattern such as the Black Spey for floating-line fishing; a clipped deerhair such as the famous Bomber for skating across the surface using a floating line, and a dry fly such as Roderick Haig-Brown's Steelhead Bee. A fly fisher can substitute many patterns for those suggested above as long as the profile matches. A Woolly Bugger or Egg Sucking Leech will do for the General Practitioner; a Woolly Worm or Black Caterpillar for the Cowichan Special; a slim-bodied sparsely dressed Skunk, Doc Spratley, Purple Peril or As Specified for the Black Spey; a Combo Bug, Lemire's Irresistible, Tom Thumb or Greaseliner for the Bomber, and a Tom Thumb, Grey Wulff or Royal Coachman for the Steelhead Bee.

The dressing for my five choices are:

General Practitioner—Orange

Hook:　　#2–#5/o low-water salmon

Tail:　　Orange polar bear hair a little longer than the hook shank and a small, red, golden pheasant breast feather

Body:　　Orange wool or seal fur

Eyes:　　Golden pheasant tippet feather

Rib:　　Medium, oval, gold tinsel

Hackle:　Orange cock neck feather wound up the body (Cut the fibres off on top so the wing can lie flat along body.)

Wing:　　Two layers of golden pheasant breast feathers with an overwing of orange-red hen neck feather extending to bend of hook

Head:　　Black Cellire varnish

General Practitioner—Black

Hook:　　#2–#5/o low-water salmon

Tail:　　Black squirrel tail a little longer than the hook shank and a small, red, golden pheasant breast feather

Body:　　Wrap hook shank with lead then black mohair or wool (Optional: Set tippet eyes in about 1/3 up body.)

Rib:　　Medium oval, silver tinsel

Hackle: Black cock neck feather wound up the body (Cut the fibres off
          on top so the back can lay flat along body.)
Back: Two layers of black spade hackles, larger black wood duck or
          black hen neck feathers, if narrow enough

I included both Orange and Black GPs because I realize that many steel-headers put a lot of faith in colour and will use only bright flies. Many years ago when I first started fly fishing for steelhead, my fly boxes, too, consisted mainly of bright orange and red flies. However, over the years I learned that fish responded better to dark patterns under most conditions. Now, of the 150 wet flies I pack around on steelhead rivers, fewer than a dozen are brightly coloured. Those few are Orange GPs and Cowichan Specials.

Cowichan Special: Red-bodied flies have been popular in British Columbia for around 75 years. One of the first was Paul Moody Smith's red-bodied, white-winged Smith's Illusion. The Cowichan Coachman was the brainchild of Cowichan River fly fisher Ron Saysell. The dressing for the Cowichan Special has changed little over its 50-year life and is:

Hook: #10–#4
Tail: A few sprigs from a white hackle
Body: Red or orange chenille
Collar: Soft, white hackle

Black Spey: There are countless flies suitable for the floating-line technique. One of my favourites is the Black Spey. Fresh in my mind is a 34-in (86-cm) summer-run steelhead that I took on a Black Spey on the Dean. That violent attack on the Black Spey and the fish's struggle to get free still has me shaking my head when I think of it. After so many years, you come to expect certain things, but every now and then an exceptional fish comes along and it's like being reborn.

The dressing for the Black Spey is:

Hook: # 2–#6 Wilson dry-fly salmon
Tip: Fine oval, gold tinsel
Butt: Black floss
Tail: Red-orange hackle tip

Body: Black floss

Rib: Medium or fine, gold twist to match hook size

Hackle: Black heron or substitute such as black-dyed pheasant rump feather

Throat: A couple of turns of teal flank feather

Wing: Bronze mallard

Head: Black Cellire varnish

Bomber: We borrowed the deerhair-clipped Bomber from our eastern Canadian Atlantic salmon-fishing counterparts for use in the skated-fly technique. Steelhead under the right water and light conditions are suckers for a fly presented this way. The dressing is:

Hook: #2–#6 Wilson dry-fly salmon

Tail: Deer hair—natural or other colours

Body: Deer hair clipped cigar shaped

Hackle: Fly tyer's fancy

Wing: Deer hair protruding over eye of hook

Steelhead Bee: Dry fly fishing for steelhead originated in British Columbia back in the 1920s on the Capilano. In the 1950s Roderick Haig-Brown experimented further with it on his home Campbell River as well as on a small summer-run stream called the Heber, a tributary to the Gold, draining to the west coast of Vancouver Island. His efforts resulted in a dry fly suited for west coast steelhead that became his signature fly. The dressing for the Steelhead Bee is:

Hook: #2–#10

Tail: Fox squirrel, quite bushy

Body: Equal sections of dark brown, yellow and dark brown wool, silk or seal fur

Hackle: Natural brown, ginger or honey, sparse

Wing: Fox squirrel, quite bushy, set slightly forward and well divided

For taking salmon in rivers the old favourites Bucktail, Mickey Finn, Muddler Minnow and General Practitioner work well. Even simpler patterns consisting of a silver body with fluorescent floss or marabou wing of pink, orange or chartreuse are popular. Other flies dressed with flashy chenille bodies of chartreuse, pink, blue, red or orange with wings of teal or mallard and with Krystal flash are the current favourites.

Sockeye, chums and pinks have recently become classed as sport fish, and on rivers such as the Fraser and Skeena with their huge runs of these species, the sport is evolving with "hot flies" being developed every day.

Fraser guide Kelly Davison has experimented over a number of years and developed a series of flies for Fraser salmon. Nicknamed KCK—Kelly's Coho Killers—they are dressed on #8–#4 hooks, have red tails, yellow or chartreuse sparkle chenille bodies, red throats, low-lying teal wings with a few strands of Krystal flash.

For coho and chinook I favour traditional patterns such as the Muddler Minnow and the Bucktail, and I would not be without the General Practitioner.

RIVER AND STREAM TECHNIQUES

There are five methods of presenting flies to fish in rivers: floating-line, skated- or waked-fly, sunk-line, dry-fly and upstream sunk-fly presentation. Summer-run steelhead and rainbow, cutthroat and brown trout are fish that may respond to all five techniques, providing the technique is married to the fish's alertness and to light and water conditions.

When observed in their river environment, most salmonids will be seen close to the bottom. British Columbia's rivers can vary in colour from what we refer to as "gin clear" to those of glacial origin with high levels of glacial flour that are almost opaque. Some rivers are so coloured that they are not worth fishing. In really silty water, you cannot catch a fish if the fish cannot see your fly, thus the popularity of flashy flies for salmon in coloured rivers such as the Fraser and Skeena system. On glacial steelhead streams I rarely go smaller than a #2 General Practitioner for sunk-line fishing, and in very silty water a #5/0 goes on the end of my line.

The sunk-line technique requires that you read the water and figure out the best angle to present your cast. Usually that is about 45 degrees downstream from where you stand, but it can vary from less than 45 degrees up to straight across from you or more upstream, depending on river flow and pool orientation. Sounds simple—just chuck it out and bring it around—but there are intricacies in river currents that make no two runs or pools identical. You need to put into the equation those variations before making your cast. There are few who are master readers of waters, but those who develop the skill catch fish most of the time.

Many river fly fishers rely solely on the sunk line as their method for catching most salmonids, and it is a staple technique to be used for many river fishes. However, there are thrilling experiences associated with the other techniques that the angler who restricts himself or herself to one technique misses out on. Moreover, sometimes fish will respond only to flies fished by another technique. Until you experience it, you do not know the thrill of seeing a fish come up and take a fly using one of the surface techniques.

The floating-line presentation is one of the most pleasant of ways to fly-fish for river fish. It is also one of my favourite methods to use for summer-run steelhead, rainbow, cutthroat and brown trout and some salmon. This method has been called "greased-line," "floating-line" and "dry-line fishing." The correct name for it is floating-line fishing. The purpose is to present a fly close to the surface with a line that floats on the surface.

In the history of fly fishing, this is a relatively new method. Devised in Great Britain in the latter part of the 19th century for Atlantic salmon fishing when clear, warm-water conditions exist, this method was popularized in the first half of this century by Arthur Wood on the River Dee at Cairnton, Scotland. The floating-line method found its way across the Atlantic and into British Columbia when Roderick Haig-Brown of Campbell River and General Noel Money of Qualicum Beach introduced it to Stamp River steelhead in the summer of 1939. Roderick Haig-Brown first wrote about it in *The Western Angler* (1939), and the method has had its devotees here since that time. I use it for summer-run steelhead on rivers when water conditions are suitable, preferably with 4–8 ft (1.2–2.4 m) of visibility and when water temperatures in the high 40s–mid-60s F (8.5–18.5 degrees C). However, I will use it for rainbows, cutthroat, browns and Dolly Varden when they are surface feeding on salmon fry or stickleback or taking other foods close to the surface. Furthermore, I have taken coho, pinks and chums in the tidal parts of rivers using this technique.

It is similar to the sunk-line technique in that an angler needs to read the water and make similar downstream and across-stream casts, except the line floats on the surface and the fly fishes just under.

In the past 15 or so years, the use of the skated- or waked-fly presentation has become increasingly popular for steelhead. However, this technique has been used by river trouters for many years. This is the last of the fly-fishing methods in which the fly is cast out either opposite you or below and brought down and across the current. With both sunk-line and floating-line presentations, the fly is below the surface of the water, but with the waked-fly method it is not. The main intent of this presentation is to dibble a fly over the lie.

This is a very old technique, dating back to 17th-century Britain. Richard Franks, speaking about Scottish Atlantic salmon fly-fishing in his book *Northern Memoirs* (1658), says, "Dibble but lightly on the surface and you infallibly raise him." Over the centuries, the waked- or skated-fly presentation has had many names. "Dibbling," "skimming," "skittering," "waking," "riffling" and "surface-lure" are some that come to mind. All refer to the method in which the fly is brought across the surface of water, causing a wake.

Summer-run steelhead and some trout respond well to this technique, providing the water clarity and light conditions suit its use. Moreover, it attracts big fish. Because of showy and at times violent rises, it is one of the most thrilling techniques used. Nonetheless, it is also one of easiest presentation techniques because all is seen. It is also a technique that fish respond to, but because the apex of the wake is at the rear of the hook fish target the apex, often missing the fly. One evening during the 1995 steelhead season, I had 10 rises of which the fly managed to get into the mouth of only three fish: I pricked one, lost one and landed one. Although fishing the waked fly is exciting, you cannot catch a fish unless you get the fly into the fish's mouth.

Furthermore, if you decide to use only this method, you have to fish it at those times of the day when light and water conditions suit its use. Water clarity of 6–8 ft (1.8–2.4 m) and subdued light of early morning, evening or areas of the river in shade suit it best. On those bright, sunlit days and particularly the afternoons under the blazing sun, exclusive use of the waked-fly method can limit your fishing day and thus your catch.

If used wisely, this is a good way of locating and catching fish. It does get the attention of travelling steelhead and other large fish. During the 1997 season on the Dean conditions remained excellent for the duration of my trip and I used this technique with a Bomber or a skated Stonefly for most of the trip. I had some fine fishing with many steelhead to 35 in (89 cm), and was delighted that I took a coho, too, on a skated Bomber. Although I have caught steelhead and trout using this technique, that coho was my first salmon.

The last two methods—dry fly and upstream sunk fly—require close work with an upstream approach to known fish-holding spots, and both techniques are more suitable to pools that hold fish. Fly fishers using the dry-fly technique will take summer-run steelhead in warmer water conditions and trout and grayling that are surface feeding on sedges, mayflies, midges or terrestrials landing on the water such as ants.

Steelhead respond probably about 90 times more readily to the waked fly over the dry fly, and many steelhead fly fishers do not make a distinction between the waked fly and the dry fly. I do. I have too deep a respect for our British fly-fishing roots and masters who preceded me to disregard the work of anglers such as George LaBranche, E. R. Hewitt and especially Roderick Haig-Brown.

The dry fly has been used in British Columbia for trout since the 1880s and for steelhead since the 1920s. Haig-Brown, who wrote about taking steelhead on dries as early as 1951, realized that fish often took the fly once it ended its drift and started to wake. In fact a dragged fly often moved fish that did not respond to the natural-drifted fly. Steelhead fly fishers were quick to adapt and ended up with the down-and-across fly presentation described earlier as the waked-fly technique.

The nymph technique is the other that favours an upstream presentation to fish in known holding waters and can be used for both winter- and summer-run steelhead, all trout and many of the province's other river game fishes.

For steelhead, this technique often works well when fish have been in a pool for a while and will not respond because they are spooky or the water has cooled and they will not rise. Often steelhead are found in deep holding pools, and this is the only technique using a weighted fly to get down to the bottom-hugging fish. For trout feeding on bottom-living insects, a fly fisher fishing a weighted nymph with a strike indicator can reap rewards.

There are variations for each method, and fishers need to keep that in mind. For example, on small rivers with pocket water I like to use a short, fast-sinking tip with weighted fly and I chuck it out and bring it through the lie. This variation marries the sunk-line and the nymph technique. Other fly fishers combine the skated and dry fly technique, by casting a little further upstream and allowing the fly to have a drift-free dry-fly float before they put the fly under tension and skate it for the remainder. Furthermore, some fish respond to a fly that is stripped. For example, cutthroats or rainbows feeding on salmon fry in slow moving water may react to a faster-moving fly. Salmon in estuaries and in slower-moving water often respond to a stripped fly. Fly fishers need to experiment.

In September 1997 I joined a group of fellow Totem Flyfishers in pursuit of Fraser pinks. I used a silver-bodied fly with a pink or chartreuse wing and a 13-ft (3.9 m) Scientific Anglers' Ultra 3 Wet Tip V line with 3 ft (0.9 m) of 10 lb (4.5 kg) test leader. With six of us sharing a 150 ft (45 m) section of water, we rotated the water and in aggregate took about two dozen pinks. Not spectacular fishing, but the really good spots are taken early on this heavily fished section of the Fraser. I managed to land about a third of the total catch. I incorporated into my sunk-line technique a 12-in (30 cm) strip, and that seemed to make the difference.

Indeed, opportunities exist on the province's rivers to use all five techniques and variations described in this discourse. Whatever method you employ, combining the right fly pattern with presentation and water and light conditions is critical for consistency.

SALTWATER TECHNIQUES

Fly fishers have been casting flies for salmon in salt water for decades. Whether it be beach fishing from shore or open ocean fishing from a boat, there are abundant opportunities for fly fishers to take salmon on the fly. Many of the estuaries and beaches along British Columbia's vast expanse of coastline have yet to see a fly fisher.

If you have equipped yourself with the #7 outfit for stillwater and the #9 outfit for large fish in rivers, you do not need to go out and buy new rods for salt water. Sink-tips like the ones recommended for river fishing and a floater are the ones preferred by most saltwater fly fishers. Big fish in the ocean can take much line and that 100 yd (90 m) of backing should be a must, perhaps more if you are after the mighty chinook or those large chums. Your reel for river fishing will suffice. However, saltwater is very corrosive, and if you use a non-anodized metal reel you should wash it in fresh water and oil it after each day's use to avoid corrosion.

Saltwater fly fishers have been catching salmon on Bucktails, Mickey Finns and flies like Mallard & Silver and Tinsel for almost three-quarters of a century, and if you have a variety of flies dressed with different coloured wings ranging in size from about 1–4 in (2.5–10 cm) you will catch your share of fish. Like flies for salmon fishing in rivers, "hot flies" are being produced and sold for saltwater. With new synthetic material appearing daily, it seems, some do prove useful, and fly tyers will be forever experimenting in search of that ultimate fly. Many do not know that it is a quest in vain as there are just too many aberrations to consider. No fly will suit all fish and all conditions.

The techniques used for saltwater fly fishing are a combination of those used for stillwater and, if you happen to hit a rip tide, those used for river fishing. However, whether you are using a floater or sink-tip in stillwater you must strip the fly. This can apply to estuary or rip tide fishing, depending on velocity of flow. Experimentation is needed to match technique. Next to summer-run steelhead I think the coho salmon is the finest game fish in the province and a thrill to get on the end of a line.

Before we review what is available through the seasons in the regions, a few words about common property and angling ethics seem appropriate. We are fortunate in British Columbia that most waters are owned by the Crown and that the public has free access to these common-property resources. However, with some anglers an intense desire to catch fish, beat others to the water and not share the water results in conflict, especially on heavily fished common-property waters. Often the resulting wrangles show humankind at its worst.

Anglers need to practice a code of ethics based on a couple of common principles such as sharing and wise use. Such things as leaving breathing room for other anglers, not trolling too close to anchored fly fishers, practicing rotation angling on streams, limiting individual catch out of hot spots and not taking more fish than your limit are a few principles that come to mind.

CHAPTER FOUR
Spring

Spring comes at different times to many of the regions in the province. By the time the most northern parts feel the warming rays of the advancing sun, the more southern parts can be experiencing summer-like weather. Nonetheless, with the sun moving over the Tropic of Cancer, its warming rays and the longer hours of daylight indicate the start of a new cycle of life in the Northern Hemisphere. There is much pleasure to be had for outdoor enthusiasts, fly fishers included, who witness this rebirth. With the warming of the earth, the deciduous trees bud, grow new leaves and some blossom. Wildflowers in a variety of colours and shapes emerge from the ground, adding extra beauty. There is new life everywhere. Shore birds and waterfowl are busy building nests and hatching young. The new broods of loons, mergansers and other ducks and geese are common sights along rivers and lakes. Spring is also the time that most fur-bearing animals give birth to their young. To many fly fishers, some who may have been cabin-bound through the long, wet or cold winter, the spring warming of the earth and water indicate the fly fishing season is about to begin.

REGION 1: VANCOUVER ISLAND

Pussy willows are one of the first signs of spring in coastal British Columbia, but there is another significant sign to the fly fisher, and that is the appearance of the salmon fry. Through the late summer and into the fall salmon migrated to their rivers of birth on their spawning run. Through the cold winter months, buried in the riverbed's gravel with clean oxygenated water sustaining the salmon's spawn, their eggs grew into little fish. In the spring they struggle from their gravel beds into the flowing river and, on many rivers, into the mouths of waiting cutthroat, rainbow or Dolly Varden. The new-born salmon are the feast of spring on rivers with trout populations.

Few Region 1 streams are prolific fish food producers. Most streams have small or no populations of resident trout. On those streams that do have resident populations, what is left is a fraction of former glory. There were just too few fish and too many anglers killing them, making the runs of river trout unsustainable. Some streams use catch and release as a management tool, while on others there is hatchery augmentation. The few rivers left that might provide the fly fisher with some sport include the Cowichan, Englishman, Little and Big Qualicum, Puntledge, Oyster, Campbell, Elk, Quatse and Salmon. Of all those rivers, the Cowichan and Elk show most promise. Because of catch-and-release management, the runs of wild trout have stabilized in past years with some reaching respectable size. However, there are streams along the west and northern coast of Vancouver Island as well as rivers on the mainland coast, some classified, that are part of Region 1 that have probably the best trout river fisheries in the region, principally because they are remote and difficult to access.

The months that a river is designated as a classified water provide an indication of the best fishing times. For example, on the Ahnuhati, Kakweiken, Kingcome and Wakeman classified season starts on April 1 and continues through to early fall. The number of guide licenses issued for classified waters is controlled by the *Wildlife Act*, but most classified waters have guided fishing opportunities. Region 1's Ahnuhati has four licensed guides, Kakweiken has five, the Kingcome three and Wakeman four.

Spring on many Region 1 steelhead streams sees the last of the winter-run steelhead. In recent years wild winter-runs have not been abundant, but all the streams mentioned above are worth a try, as are the Nanaimo, Gold, Somass, Sproat and Stamp. The Salmon River near Sayward is a late stream with winter-fish arriving fresh from the sea into May. While the Cowichan does have some late-winter fish, many steelhead that arrived as early as December are on their redds and fly fishers should avoid targeting those fish. It is just not sporting to angle for fish that are spawning.

Region 1 has a number of rivers and streams that are homes to small populations of sea-run cutthroat. It is a unique fishery often starting in the spring, with devotees who search far and wide, spend many hours learning about the fish, the estuaries, fishing beaches and best tides. Because small populations are exceptionally fragile, those who know keep secrets on location and tides to themselves. The Gorge in Victoria still has a sea-run cutthroat fishery and is an easy walk from Victoria Harbour hotels, but you need to hit it right. The more remote west and mainland coast streams in the region provide more opportunity for sea-runs.

Region 1 has about 150 to 200 lakes ranging in size from the very small to large ones such as Cowichan and Great Central, and many are regularly augmented with hatchery fish. Unlike Interior lakes, most Vancouver Island lakes are not rich in minerals that provide the foundation for aquatic life and the insect chain. Nonetheless, they do provide the spring fly fisher with opportunities, mostly for rainbow and cutthroat. Moreover, a few have kokanee, some brookies or browns, and there is the odd one with bass. Fly fishers who want to challenge the smallmouth bass head to Saltspring Island and fish Cusheon and St. Mary lakes. St. Mary has bass over 5 lb (2.3 kg) but also has cutthroat and rainbows. Spider Lake near Qualicum Beach also provides smallmouth bass fishing opportunities. Cameron, Cowichan and Somenos lakes offer browns.

Springtime is the start of saltwater salmon fly fishing season with fly fishers out in search of bluebacks. Bluebacks are coho ranging in size from less than a pound up to about three pounds (0.4–1.5 kg), most of which will form the following autumn's spawning run. Those fish will gorge themselves through the late spring and summer and be 5–10 lb (2.3–4.5 kg) and larger by the time they run to the rivers in the fall.

REGION 2: LOWER MAINLAND

The fly-fishing opportunities along the coast of Region 2 are quite similar to those in Region 1. There are no smallmouth bass or browns in Region 2, but there are sea-run cutthroat, winter steelhead and some nice Dolly Varden. Rivers such as the Vedder and the Squamish system have late-winter steelhead going into May. The Harrison, Stave and many other salmon-bearing streams offer cutthroat through the spring usually into May. Other rivers which have poorer cutthroat runs may have large Dolly Varden. Some, like those on the Squamish system, are sea-run, moving in to take advantage of the salmon fry hatch, while other rivers such as those in the Birkenhead and Lillooet system are resident.

When the freshet gets into full swing, it often determines the end of spring river fishery. But often like a poorly tuned automobile that coughs and sputters before it starts, the freshet coughs and sputters due to the unsettled weather of early spring. However, around the end of April or early May a few good days of sunshine start the snow pack melting in earnest. Often the start of the freshet draws in the last of the winter-run steelhead and with it some good fly-fishing opportunities providing the river does not rise and colour too fast. Sometimes there may be a lull in the freshet and the river can even go down. During those lulls often good fishing can be experienced, but because they are river-specific and unpredictable, local anglers usually reap the benefit.

The freshet is usually in full swing by mid-May. Large rivers with high mountains in their catchment area have much snow melt. Rivers such as the Vedder, Harrison and Squamish systems that offer Lower Mainlanders most spring fly-fishing opportunities, rise so high once the freshet starts, and on glacial fed rivers become so coloured, that the fishing is finished until the rivers recede sometime in the summer. Glacial-fed steams often remain coloured until the frosts of fall halt the glacial melt.

The northern part of Region 2 is quite inaccessible except by boat or aircraft. Some larger rivers such as the Toba, Homathko, Phillips and Southgate, Tzoonie and Vancouver offer late-winter steelhead. However, it is the cutthroat and Dolly Varden fishing on those remote streams that draw fly fishers, mostly across from Campbell River, Sechelt or Powell River, the nearest jumping-off spots.

For the lake fisher, the lower coastal lakes start fishing in early spring and the higher more inland up around Pemberton in the later months. Like Region 1 lakes, few Region 2 lakes are rich in aquatic food, but there are many lakes that provide opportunities for cutthroat and rainbows. Part-way up the coast in Region 2 lies Texada Island, and with its rich mineral deposits many of the lakes and ponds are anomalies to the general statement about Region 2's nutrient-poor lakes. Lakes such as Emily, Paxton and Priest on Texada Island offer native cutthroat in the 3–5-lb (1.4–2.3-kg) range in uncrowded settings.

For sea-run trout the Sunshine Coast, in particular the beaches north and south of Langdale and Porpoise Bay, have attracted fly fishers for years. There are many streams throughout the Sunshine Coast and inlets all the way up the Region 2 coast that offer sea-run cutthroat fly fishing opportunities. The rivers mentioned for late winter steelhead for the most part will have sea-run cutthroat. However, as with sea-run fisheries in other regions, anglers guard their secrets.

Region 2 is a huge area, and with its large population, fly fishers need to journey far afield to find absolute solitude. Even then, after hiking into a remote lake or river you may find a helicopter there and people fishing. Such is the nature of angling today.

REGION 3: THOMPSON—NICOLA

Region 3 is the land of many lakes and the home of the rainbow trout. There is a general stream closure in effect from January 1 to June 30 on most streams in this region. The regulations will tell you those that are open earlier. Some such as Cayoosh Creek and Seton River near Lillooet that have runs of steelhead have no spring closure.

Part of the Thompson, one of the finer trout rivers in the province, also has partial exemption. During May, there is a catch-and-release char and trout fishery from Canadian National Railways (CNR) Bridge below Deadman River to the CNR bridge above the Bonaparte River upstream from Ashcroft. However, with the freshet that peaks around early June, the fly fishing can be spotty. The Thompson below Savona to Lytton is a year-round classified water with no guiding permitted.

For protection from overfishing by ice-fishers during the winter months, many lakes in the region do not open until April 30, about the time that the ice comes off many of the more popular fly-fishing lakes. After a long winter under the ice in cold water, trout are eager, reckless feeders when the ice comes off. Ice-off indicates the start of the fly fishing season in the Interior. However, there are some lakes without that closure that can provide earlier opportunities. Indeed, earlier opportunities do exist, but be aware that bouts of cold, windy and snowy weather can return to this region up to the end of May.

Nevertheless, many fly fishers journey to Tunkwa, Leighton, Stump, White, Roche, Le Jeune, Peterhope, Pass, Courtney, Corbett, Salmon, Minnie, Stoney and so many other lakes in this region during May or earlier if open. Often they endure bitterly cold conditions, but at times very good early trout fishing makes this hardship worthwhile. Corbett, Minnie and Stoney are on private lands and are run as private fisheries with a fee for use. Pete McVey of Corbett Lake Country Inn offers lodging and fishing at Corbett and the Douglas Lake Cattle Ranch offers fishing and lodging at Minnie and Stoney.

If any month can be considered more reliable to the Interior trout fly fisher it is the month of June. It is usually the time of sunny, warm spring weather, not too hot, and it is chironomid time. But even better adventure awaits: as spring passes into summer the sedges start hatching and with it fly fishers can experience some of finest lake dry-fly fishing in existence.

REGION 4: KOOTENAY

With the spring closure starting on April 1 and lasting until June 14 on most Region 4 streams, the spring offers some early catch-and-release opportunities for trout and char prior to the April 1 closure. Nevertheless, the spring months are lake fishing months for the fly fisher in this region.

Lakes such as Cleland, Echo, Fortress, Horseshoe, Larchwood, Nine Bay, Premier, Summit, Tamarach, Whiteswan and others offer the fly fisher rainbow, westslope cutthroat, brookies and bull trout during the spring months. Some lakes do not open until April 30, so check the regulations. For the bass fly fisher, Kootenay Flats, Duck and Leech lakes offer some of the finest largemouth bass fly fishing in the province with fish over 5 lb (2.3 kg), while Christina, Mirror and Wasa lakes offer smaller specimens of largemouth or smallmouth bass.

Although there are opportunities for the fly fisher in this region, living way down here in Vancouver we do not hear much about good, small-lake spring fly fishing in this region. What we do hear about are the huge rainbow trout, large bull trout and kokanee, mostly taken by trollers on non-fly gear in the large lakes. However, fly fishers wanting to fish lakes such as Arrow and Kootenay can catch trout and char in these lakes if they concentrate their fishing effort on the creek mouths and use bucktails or other minnow-representing flies.

REGION 5: CARIBOO

Many fly fishers are attracted to the coastal rivers in Region 5 for the same fish that attract fly fishers to the coastal rivers of Regions 1 and 2: late winter steelhead, sea-run cutthroat trout and Dolly Varden char. The Bella Coola used to be the big draw for fly fishers, but with winter-run steelhead and cutthroat almost non-existent in recent years the only attraction now is the dollies. I recall one hour on the Bella Coola not too far downstream of the Hagensborg Airport when I took 18 nice cutthroat to 18 in (46 cm) during the early May salmon fry migration. However, there are other rivers along the many miles of Region 5's coastline such as the classified Chuckwalla, Kilbella and Nekite that are difficult to access and offer the venturous fly fisher fine spring trout and dolly fishing as well as late-winter steelhead. The Chuckwalla and Kilbella combined have four licensed guides and the Nekite five through their April 1 to May 31 classified-waters season.

Inland, up on the Chilcotin Plateau and stretching east to the boundary of Region 5, all streams tributary to the Fraser, with the exception of the mainstem, are closed from March 30 to June 30 with a few exceptions: for example, the Chilcotin has a catch-and-release fishery for steelhead from May 1 to June 15; the Horsefly is open for trout fishing from June 1; the Chilko from June 11 and the West Road/Blackwater from June 15. The Chilko has eight licensed guides, the Chilcotin also eight, the Blackwater 12 and the Horsefly five.

The Cariboo also has many fine lakes, but as in Region 3 many lakes are closed until April 30. There is usually some good fly fishing at ice-off, but, like elsewhere once you leave the coast and go inland, winter can return at any time until late May. Those venturing into the Cariboo for some early lake trout fishing may be disappointed or they may hit it right. Such are the chances for fly fishers who roll the dice.

REGION 6: SKEENA

Spring really comes to different parts of Region 6 at different times. While the Queen Charlotte Islands enjoy mild weather from the first days of spring, many of the mainland waters tributary to mighty Skeena and Fraser and northerly rivers are iced over until later in the spring.

The Queen Charlotte Islands' south island offers late-winter steelhead to the anglers plying the waters of the Copper and Pallant creeks through the spring, with a late run coming into the Deena in late April or early May. Also, Moresby Island lakes such as Skidegate Lake, White Swan and Mosquito offer native cutthroat to the fly fisher.

On Graham, the largest island in this archipelago, the Yakoun River offers steelheading, cutthroating and some rainbow trout fishing opportunities during the spring. Yakoun, Ian and Mayer lakes offer a variety of native cutthroat up to 5 lb (2.3 kg).

Many streams on the islands offer the sea-run cutthroat, the Tlell on Graham Island being one of the more famous. During the spring salmon fry migration, bluebacks (small coho salmon) venture into the Tlell estuary, and if you hit it right you can experience a truly extraordinary fishery. Anglers in search of cutthroat who venture to faraway places on Masset Inlet and Naden Harbour and many of the remoter places in the new Gwaii Haanas National Park Reserve/Haida Heritage Site will find many small streams and some estuaries with good populations of sea-runs.

The Yakoun, Copper, Datlamen, Deena, Honna, Mamin, Pallant and Tlell are classified waters through to April 30, with 10 guides licensed for Yakoun and 10 to service the other waters.

Over on the mainland in Region 6, as spring warms the waters of the streams tributary to the Skeena, life below the gravel is stirring, and when the salmon fry emerge there are cutthroat and dollies waiting. This often marks the start of the spring fishery and can occur as early as April and continue through May and in some years into June.

Many of the streams tributary to the lower Skeena, up to around Terrace, offer late-winter steelhead, cutthroat and Dolly Varden. Even the Skeena mainstem can be fished until the freshet starts, usually sometime in late April or early May. However, once the warm weather arrives the spring freshet, as well as the spring closures on many Region 6 streams, negates fly fishing in most streams. For example, all tributaries of the Skeena above Cedarvale, located about 15 miles (24 km) downstream of Kitwanga, have a winter/spring closure, as do the tributaries of the Nass. Furthermore, although both the Skeena and Nass mainstems are open, once the spring freshet gets going, the rivers, already large, swell, using the full river bed, and colour badly. This makes fishing difficult if not impossible.

Spring guided opportunities exist on classified waters such as the Ecstall with four guides licensed year-round, the Kitsumkalem with 13 guides licensed to fish from March 15 or the Kwinamass with two guides licensed year-round. There are other waters—too many to mention—that are not classified which nonetheless have guided opportunities during the spring. Furthermore, there are some waters such as the Kitseguecia, Kitwanga, Lakelse and Suskwa where guiding is not permitted at all. The Lakelse has excellent spring trout fishing and some late winter-run steelhead. The crowded Kitimat with its hatchery-augmented steelhead and cutthroat attract many anglers during the spring months.

Along the coast of Region 6 there are cutthroat lakes and other salmon-bearing rivers, mostly accessed by boat or float plane, which start to fish as spring advances. Inland, up in some of the salmon rearing lakes such as the Babine, the second largest natural lake in the province, the sockeye fry struggle from their gravelly beds into the jaws of waiting rainbows, dollies and lake trout. One of the more famous Region 6 trout fisheries, Rainbow Alley, is located at the north end of Babine Lake. This slow-moving river joins Babine with Nilkitkwa Lake and has drawn fly fishers from many places over the past 50 years to sample the large rainbow trout fly fishing during the spring salmon fry migration.

The Skeena region offers the fly fisher a variety of springtime lake opportunities, some easily accessed by road, while others, more remote, require fly-in. The farther north you go along the Stewart–Cassiar Highway, the more difficult the access. Those fisheries are best sampled when the weather is reliable in the very late spring and through the summer months.

REGION 7: OMINECA–PEACE

Region 7 is split into two management areas: 7A, Omineca and 7B, Peace. Most streams in 7A have a spring closure, but some do have partial fishing. For example, the region's only classified water, the Stellako, opens June 1, and some others have restrictive fisheries, such as the Nechako and Stuart, which are open but are catch-and-release for rainbow trout. The streams of 7B are open to angling year-round with some spring angling during mild spells, but most stream fly fishing occurs after the spring freshet from late June though into fall. These are grayling, pike and bull trout waters with some rainbows thrown in. Through May and June the rivers may be swollen with snow melt, so venturing north from Prince George to Region 7B rivers until after the spring freshet is a chancy proposition. Poor road conditions also accompany the spring thaw. The main highways and industrial roads may be fine for travel, but some of the off-beat roads to that secret lake or river spot that someone whispered in your ear can be in pretty rough shape.

Lakes in the region usually lose their ice sometime in late April or early May with the higher-elevation and more northerly ones later. There is the usual flurry at ice-off, but it takes time for the spring sun to warm the waters and get the bugs hatching. May is much more predictable for the start of lake fly fishing. Some of the salmon-rearing lakes such as Stuart and Takla have runs of sockeye. With the sockeye fry emergence in late April continuing into May there is some fine trout fishing as the fry move down into the lakes. There are numerous lakes scattered through Region 7A, such as Carp, Crystal, Emerald, Finger, Klock, Nulki, One Island and Hobson, that offer a variety of opportunities with some lakes yielding fish greater than 5 lb (2.3 kg).

Prince George fly fisher Brian Smith says there is so much fishing in the region in proximity to Prince George that he feels as if he has died and gone to heaven. For the lake fishing he recommends leech, chironomids, mayflies and bloodworms as staple patterns. Further north in Peace River country, Fisheries staff from Fort St. John recommend leeches, dragonfly, damselfly and scud imitations, with some lakes, such as Stewart, Inga and One Island, having fair chironomid activity in late May and June.

REGION 8: OKANAGAN

The land of sunshine is noted for its lake fly fishing. Lakes in the region do vary in elevation from those low-lying ones in the Okanagan Valley to those close to a mile (1.5 km) high in the surrounding mountains. The low-lying ones will come ice-free in early spring and the higher elevation ones through into late May. Rainbow trout are the target fish, shrimps, chironomids and leeches the mainstay foods, and flies representative of those insects, such as the Werner or Baggy Shrimp, Blood Leech, Woolly Bugger, Doc Spratley, Carey Special and Tom Thumb, are the staple flies. As in the Kamloops-area lakes, it is wet fly fishing most of the time, but in late spring some lakes have sedge hatches and offer dry-fly opportunities. Other lakes such as Osoyoos, Vaseaux and Christina provide spring bass fly-fishing opportunities. Some of the eastern lakes such as Quiniscue, Pyramid and Woods. all located in Cathedral Park, provide spring fly-fishing opportunities for westslope cutthroat.

Region 8 streams have a general fly fishing closure lasting until June 30. However, there are some creeks, noted in the regulations, that are open. Streams in this region flow either to the Columbia or Fraser basins. None of the Columbia basin streams has salmon other than the landlocked kokanee and as a result they do not have the abundant fry hatches that produce large fish and draw fly fishers to streams in other regions. However, some, such as the Okanagan and West Kettle, are open, offering the river fly fisher a variety of opportunities. Most of the streams that are open offer mostly small trout.

In the upper part of Region 8, which is part of the Fraser watershed, some streams do have salmon runs. The Shuswap, one of larger streams in the northern part of the region, does offer rainbow and bull trout fly-fishing opportunities through the spring. The spring freshet affects most rivers and during the rapid rise after the first hot spell most streams do not fish well until they start to recede and clear, if muddied.

Wherever you fish in the province, especially during the spring months when new regulations are issued, or if you are exploring new waters or revisiting waters after a lengthy absence, a copy of the *Freshwater Fishing Regulations Synopsis* should be your constant companion. Check what is allowed before you cast your line.

CHAPTER FIVE
Summer

Summertime is vacation time for many people. Although the sun brings out many outdoor enthusiasts, to the fly fisher summer brings new adventures and challenges. My favourite fish, the summer-run steelhead, are running, and trout fishing in rivers adds new dimensions to fly fishers' challenges. Summer weather is more stable. It is a pleasant time to race around in boats on the open ocean in search of coho, and it is also the time when early runs of salmon return to the estuaries and streams of their birth, providing big-fish opportunities. With the more stable weather and better road conditions, it is also the time for exploring remote northern waters. Yes, summertime is holiday time—fun time for the fly fisher.

REGION 1: VANCOUVER ISLAND

Anglers flock to Region 1, and have done so for decades, to enjoy salmon fishing in the sea. Some dedicated fly fishers have pursued salmon with the fly for most of this century, and the sport now called "bucktailing" evolved out of that pursuit. More and more anglers are chasing salmon on the open ocean and in river estuaries and are returning to the cast fly as their weapon of deception. Open-ocean fly fishing requires a boat in which to search for likely spots for surface-feeding coho. Tidal movement plays an important role in all sea fishing, and knowing which is the best tide may determine success or failure. In those years that I did a fair amount of coho fishing, I always preferred to fish the bottom part of the ebb, the slack and the early parts of the flood. However, local knowledge about the right time to fish what tide at what location is important. Resort and boat rental owners as well as saltwater fly fishing guides often have such information.

The importance of maps was discussed at length in Chapter 1. The same logic applies to those venturing off onto the sea as it does for those going off into the wilderness. Hydrographic charts are the maps of the sea and are as or even more important than our land maps. With hydrographic charts you can plot your course and locate sea bed depth and shoals, information that is important in picking the right spots for coho fly fishing.

For those wanting to explore for coho on their own in Region 1, the waters from about Qualicum Beach north attract the most effort, although any well-known coho haunt is worth a bet. In particular, those waters around Hornby, Denman, Lasqueti, Texada, Quadra islands and north through Johnstone Strait all the way up to Port Hardy offer opportunities to the coho fly fisher. Besides the many opportunities on the east coast of Vancouver Island, the most noted west coast coho fly fishing spots are those out of Tofino. Some resorts such as Weigh West Marine in Tofino cater to fly fishers and offer all facilities including boat rentals and guided fishing.

Open-ocean coho fishing continues through the summer, but during August and early September on the odd years there are pink salmon fly fishing opportunities for the beach fly fisher. Some well-known spots include the Puntledge, Oyster, Campbell and Eve rivers as well as rivers and estuaries in and around Port McNeill and Port Hardy.

The summer-run steelhead is one of world's finest game fish and there are a few streams on Vancouver Island that have runs of these magnificent specimens. The most famous of Region 1 rivers is the Campbell. This run provides opportunities to the fly fisher from about mid-July on. There are many other streams, such as the Tsitika and Nimpkish on the east coast and the Caycuse,

Stamp, Ash, Nahmint, Gold, Heber, Zeballos, Mahatta and Marble on the west coast, that have summer steelhead. Most populations are small, with only the hatchery-augmented Stamp's population numbering in the thousands.

Region 1 has many small rivers and streams, some of which are home to small populations of sea-run cutthroat, which migrate to the sea to grow large. Those days when rivers such as the Cowichan, Englishman, Little Qualicum, Oyster, Campbell and so many other Region 1 streams had good cutthroat populations are gone. Some fish remain, and on the right tide you will see fly fishers flinging their flies into the estuaries and beaches adjacent to cutthroat streams looking for the elusive sea-run. But it is the remote rivers and streams on the Island's west and northwest coasts and over on the mainland coast that have the most promise.

Once the weir is set and the minimum flow regime takes effect, the Cowichan, because of its regulated low summer flows, offers the fly fisher limited opportunities for browns and rainbows plus the odd cutthroat. The Elk near Campbell River provides some dry- and wet-fly opportunities through early and late summer.

Guided opportunities for trout and salmon exist on all the region's classified waters: the Ahnuhati, Kakweiken, Kingcome and Wakeman through the entire summer and on the Seymour from August 15.

The 150 to 200 lakes located in Region 1 still offer the fly fisher opportunities, but like low-lying lakes in many parts of the province the fishing goes off as the water temperature increases. Fly fishers need to pick their lake carefully with the higher level ones coming on and fishing better through the heat of summer. For the lower-altitude lakes, fly fishers need to concentrate their effort at the right times of day, with early morning or last light often being the most productive. The opportunities described in the Spring chapter remain, but because of the summer doldrums the fly fishing becomes more difficult.

REGION 2: LOWER MAINLAND

Summer fly fishing opportunities along the coast of Region 2 are quite similar to those in Region 1, although we do not have open-ocean coho fly fishing around Vancouver. Nonetheless, there are estuary opportunities at the mouth of the Capilano for coho through July and August, and in the odd-numbered years pink salmon in the Indian at the head of Indian Arm. Further north, opportunities exist along the Sunshine Coast to catch ocean-feeding coho around Thormanby, Texada and Lasqueti islands.

In the remote inlets up the coast there are some streams such as the Brem, Quatam, Little Toba and Phillips that have small populations of summer-run steelhead, but none large enough to highlight. The Chehalis and Coquihalla are the two rivers that attract the majority of fly fishers' attention in the region. However, in recent years, the Coquihalla at Hope has been closed to all fishing to protect dwindling populations, which has left Fraser Valley and Lower Mainland fly fishers only the hatchery-augmented Chehalis.

Summer is the time to explore the Toba, Homathko, Phillips, Southgate, Tzoonie, Vancouver and other streams in the many inlets along and east and north of the Sunshine Coast for sea-run cutthroat and, as summer advances, coho. The Squamish, a popular river through the spring, has headwaters originating in glaciers. Once the freshet starts it flours up and does not fish well until the freshet is finished and the river drops and clears, usually in late summer. Rivers that have salmon runs usually have Dolly Varden and the Birkenhead, Lillooet, Upper Stave and those rivers at the heads of the many inlets are worth a try if you like to catch dollies on the fly. The Harrison does not fish well during the freshet, but once river levels drop, usually from early August on, there are some prize cutthroat chasing stickleback. Catching those cutts on bright sunny days can prove frustrating, but with a Rolled Muddler or other stickleback imitation they are worth a try. Often those summer cutts are the nicest of the season. The upper Pitt Lake and Pitt River as well as the mouths of other streams flowing into the lake have fly fishing opportunities for cutts and dollies through the summer, but to get to the head of Pitt Lake requires a lengthy journey with a sturdy boat.

For the lake fisher the lower coastal lakes of Region 2, like their Region 1 counterparts, have summer doldrums. You need to pick your lake and the time of day best suited to fishing.

The Skagit, near Hope, is Region 2's prized trout stream. Conservationists waged a lengthy battle with Seattle City Light in the 1970s to protect the upper river valley from being flooded for a hydroelectric development which would have submerged this precious jewel forever. The Skagit is a catch-and-release fishery. Because of its good insect populations, trout can grow to reasonable size, with rainbows the main attraction. The stream also has bull and Dolly Varden char. The Skagit flows into Ross Lake, Seattle City Light's impoundment reservoir, and this heavily fished lake does provide fly fishers who want to keep a trout or two that opportunity.

As summer advances, the salmon runs start to return to the Fraser and other rivers in the region. As millions of sockeye and pinks—pinks odd years only—move through the Fraser they are sought by many sport fishers. Sometimes you would think that all two million Lower Mainland and Fraser Valley residents are fishing the same river. However, the Fraser is huge, and with a boat a fly fisher can usually find the odd place to cast his flies. Many, too, join the "picket fences"—rows of anglers lined up along a river bank almost elbow to elbow. If you can stand that type of fishing you will catch fish.

Chinooks are also returning to some streams in the region, with the Vedder and Chehalis and their hatchery-augmented stocks the main attraction. But when fishing the Fraser or its tributaries, if you fish deep and dirty, you never know if that salmon that takes your fly is a small pink or a huge chinook until you set the hook and you get that first run. If it is a chinook then you will be in for a long-lasting struggle, often with the fish on the winning side.

REGION 3: THOMPSON—NICOLA

Early summer is sedge time and the lake fishing in Region 3 is one of the main attractions in the late spring and early summer. Depending on elevation and location in the region, the sedge fishing lasts until about the end of July. The hatch starts on the lower lakes in June and continues up to the higher-elevation lakes until about the end of July, on those lakes that have these insects. Many of the lakes mentioned in the Spring chapter are worth a try early in the summer.

Region 3, however, does get warm in July with the hot weather often lasting through early September, then cooling as summer ends. The low-lying lakes around the 2000–3000 ft (600–900 m) level are affected most by the heat, but even then fish can be caught by altering tactics. Target the early morning and late evening and use a trolled fly to cover more water, thus more fish. Some fly fishers fish at night, especially if the lake has sedges coming off after dark. The Interior is surrounded by mountains and the higher lakes can fish well through the heat of summer. Lakes such as Arthur, Bolean, Spa, Big OK (Island), Billy, Blackwell, Blue Earth, Bulman, Calling, Dominic, Ernest, Face, Frisken, Hatheume, Hihium, Hyas, Hosli, McConnel, O.K., Paska, Pennask, Stake and others above the 4,000 ft (1,200 m) level fish better through the summer months and offer rainbows up to about 5 lb (2.3 kg). Other lakes such as Black, Fred, Tulip, Bog and McGlasken offer brook trout up to about 5 lb (2.3 kg).

The western part of the region around Lillooet and Clinton and northern parts around Barriere and Clearwater along the North Thompson offer tremendous opportunities to the lake and river fisher through the summer.

Once July starts, the general stream closure comes off, marking the start of the river trout fishing season. No matter how hot the weather becomes, the Thompson south of Savona fishes well through the summer months with trout up to 4 lb (1.8 kg), although a 4-pounder is a prize fish. The Little near Chase is another favourite trout fishery, and only a short walk or boat ride away is the world-famous Adams. Although the North Thompson can be quite silted due to glacial flour, when clear, it and the Clearwater, which join the Thompson at the town of Clearwater, offer fly-fishing opportunities for rainbow and bull trout. Other streams in the region, especially the larger ones, can provide the fly fisher with rainbow and bull trout sport. Other rivers such as the Thompson and Adams have runs of chinooks.

REGION 4: KOOTENAY

The summer months are lake and stream fishing months for the fly fisher in this region, although some of the low-lying lakes are off during the summer.

Nonetheless, as in Regions 1, 2 and 3, fish can be caught in the low-lying lakes by varying the tactics to those described for summertime fishing in Region 3. The fishing opportunities described for spring continue but with more emphasis on river fly fishing.

This region includes many lakes high in the Rocky Mountains, where summer is the time to be fishing. A ring of jewels in Mt. Assinibone Provincial Park with native cutthroat up to 10 lb (4.5 kg) includes hike-in lakes such as Cerulean, Sunburst, Wedgewood, Magog and Gog. With the peaks of surrounding mountains at the 10,000 ft (3,000 m) level, these high-elevation lakes require good hiking skills. However, we usually value those things the most for which we have worked the hardest, and a 10 lb (4.5 kg) native cutthroat from catch-and-release Cerulean Lake taken on the fly is truly a reward worth the effort. While you are in the area do not overlook the Mitchell, flowing out of Wedgewood Lake. With easy access along a horse trail, this river has many nice pools which by mid-summer offer cutthroat, bull trout and whitefish.

Yoho and Kootenay national parks in Region 4 do have some lakes and streams worth fly fishing. However, be aware that you will need a Parks Canada fishing license to fish their waters.

Late spring and early summer are freshet times, but after the rivers have peaked, and if glacial, cleared, from about mid-June onwards fly fishers can test their skills on Region 4 streams. Check the regulations to find out what is permitted on any given water. Region 4 has some of the better westslope cutthroat streams in the province. Fly fishers interested in testing their wet- and dry-fly skills against this native species should try streams such as Akolkolen, Bull, Elk and tributaries, Findlay, Fording, Goat, St. Mary, Skookumchuck, White and Wigwam. The Lower Columbia, from the Castlegar/Trail area to the American border, provides some grand sport for large rainbows and bull trout. Other streams such as the Kootenay, Palliser and Vermillion offer a variety of fly fishing opportunities for rainbows, brookies and bull trout. Region 4 offers much diversity, from pan-sized cutthroat and rainbows on smaller streams to larger rainbows and bull trout up to and sometimes over 10 lb (4.5 kg) caught from boats in B.C.'s Lower Columbia.

REGION 5: CARIBOO

Summertime in Cariboo and Chilcotin country is lake fishing time and anglers flock to the hundreds of lakes located in this huge region. There are about 200 lakes that have road access and many more that can be reached by foot, saddle-horse or float plane that provide a variety of opportunities. Some lakes have good hatches of sedges to test the angler's dry-fly skills, while others are abundant in shrimp and other aquatic insects to test your wet-fly techniques. For example, Sheridan Lake during the sedge hatch produces rainbows up to and sometimes over 10 lb (4.5 kg) to the dry fly each year, and other lakes such as Dragon and Palmer produce fish regularly in the 3 lb-plus (1.5 kg) category to the wet, with the occasional fish from Dragon going over 10 lb (4.5 kg). These lakes are only a few examples of the fine lake fishing to be had in Region 5.

In the central part of the region summertime is also the time to explore rivers. The West Road or Blackwater has gained a reputation as a fine world-class trout stream and anglers have journeyed to the Upper Dean below Anahim Lake for years to sample the trout fishing in that stream. The Quesnel, Horsefly, Cariboo, Chilcotin and Chilko are a few other big-name streams in this region that provide some excellent river trout fishing.

Many fly fishers are drawn to coastal rivers in Region 5 for the same fish that attract fly fishers to the those rivers in Regions 1 and 2: the summer-run steelhead, sea-run cutthroat and Dolly Varden. The Dean is one of finest summer-run streams in the world and anglers journey by plane, boat and helicopter to her banks though the July to September-end season. The chinooks migrating to the Dean through June and July are also attracting more fly fishers, although the river is fairly coloured with glacial flour at that time. The Bella Coola is quite coloured during the summer months, but local anglers fishing the creek mouths do take salmon in this coloured water. Chinooks return to coastal streams in all regions through the summer, but getting to them can be difficult. A guide out-fitter is probably your best bet if you are interested in pursuing chinooks with a fly on the more remote rivers.

Through the summer months guided opportunities are available for trout on the classified Chilko, Upper Dean, Horsefly and West Road/Blackwater and on the Lower Dean for summer-run steelhead.

Region 5 has a very rugged, inleted coast with streams of all sizes from small ones to large rivers. Most have salmon runs, many have cutthroat and dollies, and most provide sport through the summer in the rivers and estuaries. Especially in late summer, all along the coast the coho are migrating and congregating off the mouths of their birth rivers. If you can get to these rivers there is grand sport to be experienced. Open-ocean fly fishing for coho is also possible during the summer months, but it would take some exploring. I have not heard of fly fishers venturing into this area for that type of sport, mainly because access is so difficult. Most fishers travelling to this region's coastal waters are heading to salmon lodges whose main venues are trolling and mooching for salmon. Nonetheless, wherever salmon migrate and surface feed they can be caught with flies, and Region 5 cohoes are no exception.

REGION 6: SKEENA

Region 6 enjoys a much milder climate at this time of year than southern British Columbia and most waters fish well through the entire summer months. Summertime is the time to explore this vast region.

The lakes on the Queen Charlotte Islands continue to fish but not as well in the summer months as do the cutthroat streams mentioned in the Spring chapter. However, as summer advances from about mid-August on the pinks and coho start arriving at their birth streams with popular fly fisheries occurring at Sachs and Hans creeks and Copper River on the south island and streams in Masset Inlet and Naden Harbour on the north island. The big pink runs occur in the even years in the north country, but some northern streams have smaller runs in the odd years. In late August through the summer weeks of September, the coho will be found in the estuaries of Pallant and Copper creeks and the Tlell and Yakoun rivers and many of the other smaller coho creeks on the islands, providing some excellent sport.

Open-ocean fly fishing for coho opportunities exist off many of the creeks, sloping beaches on the east coast and around Langara Island through the summer months. Some grand sport is offered by lodges located in Naden Harbour and Langara Island for this type of coho fishing. Around Langara, sometimes large chinooks can be found feeding in shallow water near kelp beds and they, too, can be taken on cast flies. A fly fisher could spend the whole summer wandering the Islands and not tire of their fly fishing opportunities, but there are bigger and, some will say, better fish to be caught over on Region 6's mainland.

Over on the mainland, the big chinooks are returning to the Skeena, her tributaries, and other large rivers along the coast. If fly fishers want to challenge a 50-lb (22.5 kg) monster this is the place to go. However, the Skeena is a huge river and best fished with a jet boat. Remember, you need to bring big flies and use stout tackle for those monsters. The Kitimat offers a different type of experience with its hatchery-augmented chinooks. You will fish in a much smaller river, which can be safely drifted or walked. It is crowded, though.

Many of the streams tributary to the Lower Skeena, up to around Terrace, continue to fish well through the summer months for cutthroat and Dolly Varden. The Lakelse and Kitimat offer the fly fisher some excellent cutthroat fishing, and other streams offer cutthroat and some good dolly fishing, especially if salmon are spawning. Cutthroat, dollies and whitefish will lie a little downstream of spawning salmon, taking eggs that are taken out of the redd by the current. One successful technique consists of casting a salmon egg pattern similar to the Cowichan Special upstream, letting it drift through the spawning fish, then striking when the indicator either goes down or moves upstream. In late summer the coho are starting to move into their parental streams offering some good sport, the Lakelse being one of the better fly fishing coho streams. Even the crowded Kitimat is worth a try for those scrappy fish.

It is, however, the summer-run steelhead returning through August and September that draws fly fishers from around the globe to Region 6's classified streams. Streams such as the Copper (Zymoetz), Bulkley, Morice, Bear, Kispiox, Babine, Suskwa and Sustat as well as the Skeena mainstem are fabled rivers in the world of the summer-run steelhead fly fisher. Guided opportunities exist on all these rivers with the exception of the Suskwa.

The summer steelhead runs move through the Lower Skeena and into its tributaries through August and September. With optimum water temperatures they provide excellent sport, with surface presentations being favoured by fly fishers. Some steelhead, on the Kispiox particularly but on other rivers as well, exceed the 20 lb (9 kg) mark frequently. There are few thrills in the world of fly fishing equal to a large steelhead taking a surface-presented fly.

Although both the Skeena and Nass mainstems are open, once the spring freshet gets going, the rivers, already large, swell, using the full river bed, and colour badly, making fishing difficult. However, once the freshet peaks and the river starts to recede and the huge gravel bars start to show, it is worth throwing in a fly. Some of the gravel bars on the Skeena are so huge that you could spend the whole day just fishing one properly.

Along the coast of Region 6 the cutthroat lakes, mostly accessed by boat or float plane, continue to fish throughout the summer. Inland, the lake and river trout fisheries fish well through the season. Babine, Ootsa, Francois and other large lakes that have few access points are best accessed by plane or if time permits a large boat. If you can afford it, exploring areas such as the difficult-to-access watersheds of the north country is best done with a good guide outfitter. Not only will it save you time, but also the guides have already done much of the exploring and will get you into the best places when the fishing is at its best, weather permitting.

It matters not which region or whether you are fishing a river, lake or sea, adverse weather such as wind, rain, snow and cold can affect the fishing, sometimes for only a day but often for much longer.

A number of years ago I remember arriving at the Kispiox and taking three steelhead that afternoon. That night the rains came. We spent the rest of the week driving around the different rivers looking for fishable water, eventually finding only the Skeena below the confluence with the Kitwanga worth fishing. Yes, storms can and do disrupt fishing trips.

There are many waters in Region 6 to explore, but none is probably as good or famous as the easily accessible Babine's Rainbow Alley, which offers dry- and wet-fly trout fishing for fish up to 10 lb (4.5 kg) through the summer.

No doubt the waters of the Skeena and the Queen Charlotte Islands attract most of fishers heading into Region 6. Nonetheless, there is a whole new world waiting for those venturing north along the Stewart–Cassiar Highway. Rainbow trout and char in lake and stream and grayling and pike in the northernmost waters provide opportunities in this little populated area. Summer is the time to be exploring those watersheds. My friend Rob Brown, who writes "The Skeena Angler" column for the *Terrace Standard*, has wandered along the Stewart–Cassiar Highway testing the waters. During the 1997 summer he spent some time working with a fisheries consultant inventorying streams tributary to Atlin Lake. Rob, a keen fly fisher, sampled the waters with rod and line and reported grayling to over 20 in (50 cm). He recommends highly the northern part of Region 6 not only because of the good fishing in wilderness settings but also because of the grand scenery.

However, the farther north you go along the Stewart–Cassiar the more difficult the access. But perhaps we should think of those opportunities differently because often those places more difficult to get to offer the most surprises.

REGION 7: OMINECA–PEACE

Over 200 years ago, when the first explorers came to what is now Region 7, they did their exploring after the spring ice-out. They found they endured severe hardships travelling on rivers swollen with snow melt that would have been much easier to navigate during the lower flows of summer and fall. Even with improved access into the northern parts of Region 7, summer, after the freshet has peaked and is receding, remains the best time to explore these streams.

The streams of 7A offer a variety of opportunities to the fly fisher. The Fraser mainstem around Valemont, Crooked, McCloud, Nechako, Cheslata, Endako, Stuart and Tachi all offer rainbows and bull trout. As well, the Stellako, which is a fly-fishing-only stream, offers rainbows to about 7 lb (3.2 kg). The Stellako is a classified water and with only one guide licensed for this water it provides limited guiding opportunities. The Mesilenka has some phenomenal Arctic grayling with fish in the 20-in-plus (50 cm) range as well as large rainbows and bull trout. The Nation near Mackenzie has good rainbow and grayling fishing, but there are many streams tributary to Williston Lake for anglers to explore for Arctic grayling, rainbows and bull trout.

Region 7 covers a huge territory. I quizzed a friend who is based in Prince George, which is in 7A, whether he had explored any waters in 7B. He confessed he was not that familiar with the other half of the region. There was so much fine fishing in his area, why would he travel all that way? Looking at a map of the area with all the lakes and streams within a 150-mi (250-km) radius, I can easily understand his attitude.

Region 7 north of Fort St. James and Mackenzie is grayling country, but anglers will also find rainbows in some waters and bull trout in many more. There are thousands of miles of rivers to explore in this immense region. Rivers such as the Nation, Omineca, Mesilinka, Pelly-Ingenika draining into Lake Williston, the Parsnip and its tributaries, the tributaries of the Laird such as Kechika, Toad, Coal, Smith, Racing, Testa, Muskwa and Prophet, the Peace itself, the Pine and its tributaries the Murray and Sukunka, the Burnt, the Sikkani Chief along the Alaska Highway, the Buckinghorse and the Prophet all offer the fly fisher sport with grayling. The rivers with the biggest insect populations will grow the largest grayling. However, they will also be the rivers where insects bother you most. Don't forget the bug repellent.

Lakes throughout the region fish well through the summer, some offering rainbow, others grayling, and many bull and lake trout char.

This region is so vast with so many wilderness waters that you might want to seek out a guide outfitter. There are about 30 licensed guides in this region who provide a wide variety of choices from comfortable lodges to horseback and camping adventures. Logging roads do provide some access, but many streams are in the wilderness, and some probably have yet to see a fly cast on their pools. For those with limited funds there are a number of provincial parks and forestry campsites throughout the region. Fishing vacations can certainly be enjoyed by moving from location to location and testing the waters yourself.

REGION 8: OKANAGAN

Fresh water and sunshine draw tourists by the tens of thousands to Region 8. However, the days of constant sunshine and hot temperatures really put the low-lying lakes into the summer doldrums. Nevertheless, even on low-lying lakes those waters mentioned in the Spring chapter can be fished if you pick the right time of day. However, if you want more than a couple of hours of fishing a day, you will need to concentrate your efforts on the higher elevation lakes that do not start to fish well until the summer heat has warmed their waters. Region 8 has many lakes over 4,000 ft (1,200 m) elevation, and lakes such as Aberdeen, Aileen, Beaver, Boileau, Brenda, Brunette, Dee, Doreen, Eneas, Fishhawk, Island, Kentucky, Loon, Meadow, Nicklen, Siwash, Skunk, St. Margaret, the private-access, reservation-only Teepee lakes, Friday, Saturday and Sunday lakes and many others offer a variety of fly fishing for rainbows up to about 5 lb (2.3 kg). Some high-level lakes have easy access on good secondary roads, others require four-wheel drive and some are hike-in. Know where you are going before starting out.

For the brook trout fly fisher, try lakes such as Becker, Christie, Idabel, Keefer and Postill, to name a few, that fish well through the summer for fish up to 3 lb (1.4 kg).

Region 8 is laced with small streams, most with small trout. You can try your hand at catching them, wandering around along small streams on beautiful summer days. There are, however, a couple of larger streams that offer the fly fishers far more than pan-sized trout. The Kettle, one of the streams stocked with brown trout decades ago, besides browns, has rainbows, brookies and whitefish, and its sister stream, the West Kettle, all but browns. The Shuswap along its many miles is noted as having excellent fly fishing for rainbows, and fly fishers may also catch bull trout and whitefish.

Summer brings the fly fisher many new and exciting opportunities: from salmon in the sea, summer-run steelhead in coastal rivers, grayling in the north to rainbow, brookies and cutthroat in the high-elevation lakes. However, if I had to restrict myself to a six-week season to fish, my choice would be the last two weeks of September and the month of October—the early fall.

CHAPTER SIX
Fall

In the Northern Hemisphere spring is the season of rebirth, summer the time of plenty, and fall is the time that the earth goes back to sleep. The spring-born young of animals have grown large enough to face the onslaught of winter. Birds and waterfowl, which journeyed north to breeding grounds in British Columbia to hatch and raise their young, in the fall migrate south to winter feeding grounds.

The salmon that returned in abundance through the late summer and fall are busy digging nests and depositing the next generation; then they die. When Europeans first noticed the massive numbers of dead salmon along the river banks, they pondered the waste. However, in Nature there is little waste. It is true that pinks, chums, sockeye, coho and chinooks die after spawning. But the return of the salmon to the river is the beginning not the end. From time immemorial, the runs of salmon have been the basic food of the First Nations and sustained them through the bleak winter months. The salmon, too, on the spawning grounds provide food for many animals, and bears in particular rely on that abundance to get them ready for their winter hibernation. The masses of dead salmon as they decay are the beginning of life, providing nutrients to insects and zooplankton, which in turn feed the hungry salmon fry when they dig out of their gravel beds in the spring. Yes, the returning hordes of salmon and their collective deaths are truly a paradox: from death comes life.

Fall is a season of change. Along the coast the fall storms entice the salmon into the rivers. Deciduous trees bring new beauty to the landscape with aspen, birch, cottonwood and vine maple leaves a changing rainbow of colour. The long hot days of summer pass. But often, when we have an Indian summer, the sunny days remain but with cooler nights and frosty mornings. The mountains crowned with freshly fallen snow add even more beauty.

All along the coast and in the interior of the province fall provides some of the best fly-fishing opportunities a fly fisher could wish for. One year, I thought I would scoot up to the Coquihalla and fish the last couple of days of the season. Late September in the upper Fraser Valley can be very pleasant, but the nights can be cool and frosts common. The Coquihalla was low, clear and on the cool side, the sort of conditions that put summer-run steelhead into deep holding pools. I found one steelhead holding behind a large boulder slick in one the river's many chutes. When I first spotted her she was near the tail of the slick, but because I was walking upstream along the edge of a high bank as I noticed her, she saw my movement through her window and scooted for cover. I left her to settle down and returned later but could not get her to take.

The next morning when I returned, she was near the slick's tail. This time I decided I would use the upstream-nymph technique from the gravel bar on the other side of the river. I tied on a #8 Cowichan Special and approached cautiously. One mistake and I knew she would run for cover. However, things clicked this morning and it was only a cast or two later that I noticed the float-ing part of my leader halt and move a little upstream. I struck and eventually landed a small 22-in (56 cm) female steelhead. Certainly, that 22-incher was one of my smaller steelhead but quite a challenging one to catch. Conditions deteriorated and I thought I would drive to the Skagit for the night flight. No sooner had I arrived, got my trout gear ready and waded the pool when a hatch of large duns started coming off. The river that appeared barren of life when I arrived was now a hot house of activity with trout rising everywhere. What to use? I quickly scanned by my box of dries and chose a #8 Grey Wulff. Little did I know that the hatch would finish as quickly as it started. In just over half an hour it was over, but I did manage to hook four trout, with a 14½-incher (37 cm) the largest.

Days fishing are remembered for different reasons. On my previous trip to the Coquihalla, in five hours on the river I was into 16 steelhead and rainbows, but taking one steelhead on the nymph-technique in the Coquihalla and later the rainbows from the Skagit on the dry-technique to me culminated an almost perfect day. Using knowledge earned through years of experiences, studying the masters, honing the skills and having the ability to size up different river and light conditions to make sound decisions that end up with fish on the beach symbolize to me what fly fishing is all about.

REGION 1: VANCOUVER ISLAND

The fly-fishing opportunities of summer continue though the fall, with salmon being the main attraction. The coho are homing on their parent streams through late September into October and are followed by the chum. Fly fishers should target the salmon haunts mentioned in the Summer chapter. Cowichan and Duncan bays in years past used to be world famous and attracted many anglers. The province's largest coho, a massive 31-pounder (14 kg), was taken from Cowichan Bay on October 11, 1947. Charlie Stroulger, a long-time Duncan fly fisher who has lived on Cowichan Bay since the 1920s, remembers well the abundant runs and the fabulous fly fishing. However, when I visited him in the spring of 1997 and we looked over the bay from his home, talking about the good old days, he lamented that the fishery he knew so well and loved is now a tiny fraction of what it used to be. Farther north, the Elk Falls pulp mill dominates the Duncan Bay landscape, and that fishery, too, has suffered greatly.

No matter what coastal water, weather determines the kind of fall fishery we enjoy for salmon. If we have a long-lasting Indian summer with rivers on the low side, coho and chum runs are more reluctant to move upriver en masse so trickle through providing more fly-fishing opportunities along the beaches, estuaries and in some of the larger rivers.

By fall, all Region 1's summer-run steelhead will have entered their streams. Some would have been in fresh water as early as June, perhaps some even as early as May. Often, in low, clear, summer flows, steelhead can become dour and are poor takers. A fall rain, however, often freshens up the water. As the river drops the fish can become quite active, and many of those streams mentioned in the Summer chapter are worth a try.

In the fall the sea-run cutthroat homes on its mother stream, often following the coho. They enter fresh water with the salmon but unlike the salmon not to spawn but to eat salmon eggs.

Guided opportunities for trout and salmon exist on all the region's classified waters: the Ahnuhati, Kakweiken, Kingcome, Wakeman and Seymour through to October 31.

In addition the Cowichan becomes refreshed with the fall rains and is worth a try for salmon and trout. Fly fishing usually perks up on the lakes.

REGION 2: LOWER MAINLAND

Fall fly fishing opportunities along the coast of Region 2 are quite similar to those in Region 1. The lakes fish better through the fall after the summer doldrums, and the summer-run steelhead does provide some sport in the streams mentioned in the Summer chapter. During the fall, as water temperatures drop, especially on low, clear streams, it becomes more difficult to get fish to rise to your fly. You will have to fish down to them.

It is the runs of salmon that attract the attention of most fly fishers in the fall. For Vancouver and Fraser Valley anglers, the Harrison and Vedder with their hatchery runs show the most promise. If the rains have not yet set in, salmon will move en masse through the Fraser and hold off their home streams awaiting a rise in water. Thus they may be susceptible to an enticing fly. However, if the rains have already swollen the rivers, the salmon will shoot right through into their home streams, providing fewer opportunities for the angler.

In the inlets up the coast, streams such as the Brem, Clowholm, Rainy, Skwanka, Theodosia, Tzoonie and Vancouver have runs of coho and cutthroats through into November. Glacial-silted streams such as the Squamish,

Cheakamus and Mamquam clear with the frosts of early fall, and their runs of coho and chum are worth a try through October into November.

Cutthroat, coho and chums migrating to other streams tributary to the Pitt River and Pitt Lake can provide fly fishing opportunities. The Stave below Ruskin Dam has coho, chums and cutts.

The Fraser near Chilliwack is worth a try as coho and chums migrate through to other rivers. The last of the steelhead runs destined for Upper Fraser tributaries such as the Thompson and Chilcotin pass through the Lower Fraser in early fall, and who knows what you might catch. But remember, all wild steelhead in Region 2 must be released.

For the Skagit trout angler, keep in mind that small streams like the Skagit cool rapidly on cool fall nights. If there is to be a hatch of flies, it will occur after the river has warmed through the day and may be of short duration. For the Skagit River and Ross Lake fly fisher, both fisheries close on October 30.

REGION 3: THOMPSON—NICOLA

Some of the finest lake fishing takes place in the fall in this region, often under less crowded conditions. For many fly fishers in British Columbia, fly fishing opportunities in the winter are few, and as spring comes anglers show unabated enthusiasm. However, for many, after enjoying the lakes and rivers through the warm summer days, their enthusiasm wanes with the colder nights and cooler days of fall. Too, come fall many fly fishers are in pursuit of other fish such as salmon and steelhead, while others enjoy hunting and are after big game, upland bird or waterfowl. The net effect is fewer anglers on the lakes during a time when fish feeding activity is great.

I do not know if fish sense that the season of plenty is coming to an end and that they may be spending many months under ice-covered water, but anglers journeying into Region 3 during the fall months can enjoy some grand fishing. The reverse to the spring-summer conditions is in effect: high-altitude lakes cool and freeze earlier and low-lying ones much later. Chironomids, shrimps, leeches and water boatman are the target foods and fly fishers patterns representative of those foods are best.

Stream fishing continues through the fall with smaller streams cooling quicker. In cold water trout are less active and become less inclined to feed. Big rivers such as the Thompson cool much more slowly and have good trout fishing temperatures often through October, but once November comes the river has cooled enough that trout can become difficult to catch.

During the late summer, one of the world's hardest-fighting game fish has entered the Fraser and, after journeying 200 or more miles (about 300 km), they start to arrive in the Thompson around Spences Bridge in early to mid-October. Those mighty Thompson summer-run steelhead attract anglers from throughout the fly-fishing community, with fishers from Europe even making the journey to test their skills. The last couple of weeks of October and the first two of November are more reliable, but after mid-November, sometimes earlier, it can get quite cold. I remember one year in the mid-1980s when the temperature plummeted to about -4 degrees F (-20 degrees C) on October 31 and snow fell. The routes out of the area were closed to travel. It was too cold to fish, and once the weather broke the exodus began. However, like many early cold spells this one was not long lasting. I managed to get to the Thompson, a classified, non-guided river, in between snow storms. Because all the other anglers had left I had a river to myself and caught some fine steelhead.

REGION 4: KOOTENAY

The fall months see the continuation of lake and stream fishing for the fly fisher in this region, with the high-level, Rocky Mountain lakes and streams affected earlier by the cooler fall days. Like other lakes and rivers in other regions, fall temperatures, altitude and size of water determine how quickly water temperatures drop and when fish become difficult to catch. For example, if you are a die-hard angler and wanted to fish well into the fall and sample different experiences, you would target the higher-altitude small lakes and streams in the early fall. As the fall season and colder weather advanced, you would move to the larger lakes and rivers and later move down into the valley bottoms where some of the larger waters remain ice free and available to anglers year-round.

REGION 5: CARIBOO

Not as many lakes in this region are affected by the summer doldrums, but as in other regions the trout fly fishing can be excellent with the higher lakes affected earlier by the cooler fall temperatures.

Region 5 has a number of classified rivers, some with a limited season. Those seasons often will tell fly fishers what time is best. For those with fall fisheries, the end of the season is often the end of the comfortable fishing weather, although local anglers can and do take advantage of mild spells much later. For example, on the West Road or Blackwater, Upper Dean below Anahim Lake, Horsefly and Chilko the classified-water season ends on October 31. From that anglers can assume that trout fishing in those streams is good until that date, weather permitting. It is also a hint that the trout fishing season in non-classified rivers such as the Quesnel, Cariboo, Canim, Mitchell and many others will continue through to the end of October, weather depending.

With the classified Lower Dean closing on September 30, it provides limited fall summer-steelhead and salmon fishery. Many streams along Region 5's rugged coast will have coho, chums, cutthroat and Dolly Varden or bull trout fisheries through October, possibly into November. However, other than those in the Bella Coola valley and some with logging road access, water or air travel to those waters is hampered by fall storms. Nonetheless, rivers in the Bella Coola system, if the coho run is good, have fair coho, cutthroat and dolly fishing. The glacial melt that feeds the Bella Coola through the summer months stops in the fall, and with clearer water the river becomes a better prospect for fly fishers.

REGION 6: SKEENA

Although the cutthroat in the lakes on the Queen Charlotte Islands are waiting for the fly fisher to cast a stickleback imitation such as a Rolled Muddler their way, the coho and cutthroat river fly fishing are the big attraction through the early fall. As fall advances and nears its end, the early winter-run steelhead start to show in rivers such as the Yakoun and Copper. Again, as in Region 5, the classified-river season on streams such as the Yakoun, Copper, Datlemen,

Honna, Mamin, Pallant and Tlell provide an indication that there is fishing through the fall, first for coho and cutthroat and later for steelhead.

Over on Region 6's mainland, the coho and cutthroat are returning to coastal streams all along the coast and to the inland tributaries of the large river systems. The summer-run steelhead streams such as the Copper (Zymoetz), Bulkley, Morice, Bear, Kispiox, Babine and Sustat as well as the Skeena mainstem are the main draws for anglers journeying into Skeena country. Most of those streams are classified with a season end of October 31. That date is a good hint that in late October the region can get cold and, although local anglers can take advantage of lulls in the cold weather and fish till the rivers close December 31, visitors should be wary of planning trips into Region 6 after October.

Along the coast of Region 6, the cutthroat lakes and rainbow lakes continue to fish through the fall. Lakes under the influence of coastal weather patterns will fish much longer while those inland and more northerly waters provide the best opportunities through the early fall. Mid-to-late October is roughly the end of the inland lake fishery. Waters in the upper part of the region, along the Stewart–Cassiar highway and those up around the Atlin area, will fish into October. However, snow can come at any time after September-end, so be aware before venturing off into faraway places on back roads in the fall.

REGION 7: OMINECA–PEACE

There are no new fishing opportunities in this region that are not discussed in the Summer and Spring chapters. Lake and river fisheries for rainbow, bull trout, pike, Arctic grayling, brook trout and whitefish continue through the fall with the more northerly parts of the region's season ending in early October and the more southerly later. Winter can strike at any time in this country after October sets in. However, the fly fishing will continue until the first sheets of thin ice cover the lakes. Few waters in this region survive the long cold winter ice free.

REGION 8: OKANAGAN

The days of sunshine and roses continue in this region through the fall. Few years are without the Indian summer that coastal regions long for and so enjoy when they experience one. Lake fishing continues to be the main draw, and as in Region 3, the high-level lakes are affected first by the cooler fall nights. However, there is good fly fishing to be had on lakes through fall, often into November, weather permitting.

The streams and rivers lacing Region 8 continue to provide trout fishing opportunities through October, depending upon the size of the waterbody. Streams with large headwater lakes cool more slowly and provide fishing opportunities later.

In summary, fall fishing throughout the province continues to provide many challenges, some continuing from the summer and some new to the fly fisher. However, as fall progresses, the leaves turn colour and fall, the lakes and streams cool, the salmon die, the birds fly south, some animals go into hibernation, and with good opportunities for fly fishing diminishing many anglers hang up their rods as most regions of the province go to sleep.

CHAPTER SEVEN
Winter

Winter is the time for hibernation and a time of survival for many creatures living in British Columbia. Rivers and lakes cool. In cold water fish become semi-dormant and are not on the move hunting for things to eat. All seasons vary over British Columbia's vast landscape, but perhaps the greatest difference is in the winter. Coastal communities usually have relatively mild weather, while many of the inland and more northerly regions are in a deep freeze. Winter days can be bleak and cold and daylight short. Because of these factors, winter fly fishing opportunities through the dead of winter, if present at all, are difficult. For the majority of fly fishers, winter is the time to replenish the fly box depleted by those trips after trout, salmon and steelhead through the more productive seasons. There remain a few fly fishing opportunities for the hearty adventurer. Most opportunities are on waters mentioned in the other three seasons.

REGION 1: VANCOUVER ISLAND
All along the coast, winter steelhead are on the final leg of their many-month sea-journey and are returning to natal streams, many destined for streams in Region 1. Poor runs in recent years have made steelhead fly fishing more

difficult. In cold water steelhead will not move far to take a fly, so a fly fisher must get down to them to fish effectively. The deep slow pools that winter fish often prefer provide challenges. With poor returns in recent years, wild winter-runs are not abundant, but the Cowichan, Nanaimo, Englishman, Gold, Somass, Sproat, Stamp, Little and Big Qualicum, Oyster, Campbell, Salmon, Nimpkish, Woss, Quatse and Keogh are all worth a try. Over on the mainland coast the Ahnuhati, Kakweiken, Kingcome, Wakeman and Seymour also provide winter fly fishing opportunities. The best time to fish winter steelhead is after a good rain when the river is falling and, if coloured, as it clears.

Summer steelhead that enter a river during July to September remain in the river until the following spring spawning season and are relatively easy to catch in streams such as the Stamp and Campbell. Some anglers frown on fishing for these fish and the few I have taken from the Campbell put up a poor fight. Some steelhead on the Campbell have been caught so many times through the summer and fall that is seems they know that the quickest way to get that thing out of their mouth is not to struggle but swim to shore where an odd-smelling, five-fingered thing will remove the annoyance from their mouth.

Winter fish begin showing in some rivers such as the Cowichan and Campbell as early as December, with the peak of the runs occurring through February and March on many streams. Some runs peak even later.

There is some trout fishing available in many of the same streams mentioned in other chapters. Cutthroat do follow the salmon into the rivers in the fall with many wintering in their parental streams, spawning in the spring. However, other than those streams over on the mainland trout fishing is a chancy proposition through the dead of winter. Sea-run cutthroat are an all-year fish and opportunities do exist along some beaches and estuaries of Region 1. As winter wanes, though, giving way to spring, river water temperatures rise and trout fishing does improve. The Cowichan with its browns, rainbows and cutthroats is the best bet for trout fishing of all Region 1 streams.

Even those living on Vancouver Island experience varying degrees of winter with the more southerly parts often much milder than the upper half, from Courtenay north. Only in the coldest of winters do the lakes freeze, and although Region 1 lakes are not prolific fish food producers, there are some fly-fishing opportunities. Chironomid hatches occur as early as February and flies based on this insect are among the more successful used during the early parts of the season. In the southern part of the region from about Nanaimo south, the lower the lake elevation the earlier the water warms and bugs start to hatch, providing fly fishing opportunities. Also worth a try on the milder days of winter are the bass lakes on Saltspring Island.

REGION 2: LOWER MAINLAND

Winter fly fishing opportunities in Region 2 are similar to those of Region 1. Winter steelhead return as early as December. Rivers that have easy access are the most popular, with the Vedder/Chilliwack system runs showing first and the Squamish system later in the winter. Most steelheaders pick rivers with easy access to fish during the dead of winter.

The Fraser, its sloughs and main tributaries such as the Pitt do provide cutthroating opportunities through the winter, as does Pitt Lake. The Fraser is the more reliable, providing the river is clear and free from ice. Region 2 lakes do provide some opportunities in late winter. The shallower, low-level ones are more reliable, chironomid flies being recommended. Some anglers even take cutthroat fishing chironomids on the Fraser sloughs during winter.

Opportunities do exist all along the coast during the winter for winter steelhead, sea-run cutthroat and Dolly Varden. However, travelling long distances into remote waters during the winter to fish what can be a very short day has its drawbacks. More and more anglers are using helicopters to explore remote waters. You get there quickly and are able to fly from place to place, but it is costly. See the Spring chapter for possible streams.

REGION 3: THOMPSON–NICOLA

Many of the prime trout lakes of this Interior region have a winter closure lasting from December 1 through to April 30 to protect stocks from overfishing by ice fishers. Because of the cold winters in this region there are few angling possibilities. The Thompson below Savona provides limited steelhead fly fishing through the last of the year until it closes December 31. Rivers near Lillooet may provide local anglers with steelhead opportunities as runs wintering in the Fraser move up and into their natal streams for the spring spawning.

During mild spells there may be the opportunity to throw a line into some of the rivers in the region for whitefish and perhaps even catch the odd rainbow and bull trout, moreso as winter wanes in March. Some low-lying lakes not covered by the winter closure may start to fish in very late winter. Local anglers are best suited to take advantage of mild spells and subsequent angling opportunities during the winter. Other than the Thompson during late December, the times to fish Region 3 are from about May to October and certainly not December through March.

REGION 4: KOOTENAY

Fly fishing opportunities through the winter months in this region are dependent on the severity of winter. Many lakes are closed to protect stocks from overfishing by ice fishers and all streams have a catch-and-release limitation on bull trout from November through March. Nonetheless, there are large bodies of waters such as Kootenay, Slocan and Arrow lakes that remain ice free through the winter, and some of the larger rivers provide some fly fishing opportunities. With low water temperatures and sluggish fish, winter fly fishing is tough. Techniques used for winter steelhead fishing provide the most promise.

REGION 5: CARIBOO

The interior of this region is cold country during winter with few fly fishing opportunities. Unless you live nearby and can take advantage of mild spells you certainly do not travel into this part of Region 5 in the winter. However, along the coast, winter steelhead, Dolly Varden and cutthroat opportunities exist with late winter providing the more reliable opportunities. The Bella Coola was the big draw in years past, but its steelhead, cutthroat and dolly fisheries are a mere fragment of former years. Wintertime is not the time to be exploring the more remote waters of Region 5.

REGION 6: SKEENA

Of all the waters in British Columbia, it is those of the Queen Charlotte Islands that show the most promise for winter fly fishers. Winter steelhead are the big draw with the Yakoun and Copper rivers and Pallant Creek having the most fishing pressure. Those streams also have wintering cutthroat and the occasional Dolly Varden.

The lakes on the Islands do not freeze and cutthroat can be taken on the low-lying ones, with late winter the best bet.

Over on Region 6's mainland, some coastal streams and some in the Lower Skeena valley provide most of the winter opportunities. Rob Brown of Terrace related to me a story of a time he and some friends went to the Lower Copper (Zymoetz) to capture and tag winter steelhead. With ice flowing down the river, conditions could not be worse, but they did catch fish with the fly out-producing the bait on this occasion. Weather permitting there are winter steelheading, cutthroat and Dolly Varden opportunities on many of the rivers tributary to the Lower Skeena, including the Skeena mainstem. However, as in many places in British Columbia, anglers living nearby are best able to take advantage. You would not plan a trip to fish the Copper in January—weather and conditions are just too chancy.

The northern part of the region is usually in a deep freeze during winter. Unless you can devise a way to fish a fly through a hole in the ice there are no fly fishing opportunities to speak of.

REGION 7: OMINECA—PEACE

This region, because it is well inland and extends north, has the severest winters of all regions. Fly fishing opportunities are virtually non-existent through the winter months.

REGION 8: OKANAGAN

This region provides few fly fishing opportunities through the winter months. Some streams may offer whitefish or bull trout to those wanting to feel something tugging on the end of their line. There may be a few lakes exempt from the December 1 to April 30 ice-fishing closure that may provide some sport as winter wanes in March. However, like other interior regions, venturing forth into Region 8 expecting to find good fly fishing in winter is unrealistic.

Appendix A

Species Availability for the Fly Fisher Per Region Per Month, Tidal and Non-tidal Waters

Species	Jan.	Feb.	Mar.	Apr.	May	June	July	Aug.	Sept.	Oct.	Nov.	Dec.
Rainbow Trout		1	1, 2, 3, 4, 8	All	All	All	All	All	All	All	1, 2, 3, 4, 8	1, 2, 3, 6
Steelhead Trout	1, 2, 3, 5, 6	1, 2, 3, 5, 6	1, 2, 3, 5, 6	1, 2, 3, 5, 6	1, 2, 3, 5, 6	1, 2, 3, 5, 6	1, 2, 5, 6	1, 2, 5, 6	1, 2, 3, 5, 6	1, 2, 3, 5, 6	1, 2, 3, 6	1, 2, 3, 6
Cutthroat Trout	1, 2, 5, 6	1, 2, 5, 6	1, 2, 5, 6	1, 2, 3, 4, 5, 6, 8	1, 2, 3, 4, 5, 6, 8	1, 2, 3, 4, 5, 6, 8	1, 2, 3, 4, 5, 6, 8	1, 2, 3, 4, 5, 6, 8	1, 2, 3, 4, 5, 6, 8	1, 2, 3, 4, 5, 6, 8	1, 2, 3, 5, 6	1, 2, 3, 5, 6
Brown Trout		1	1	1, 8	1, 8	1, 8	1, 8	1, 8	1, 8	1, 8	1, 8	
Brook Trout Char		1	1, 2	1, 3, 4, 8	All	All	All	All	All	All	1, 2, 3, 4, 8	
Dolly Varden or Bull Trout Char	1, 2, 5, 6	1, 2, 5, 6	1, 2, 5, 6	1, 2, 5, 6	1, 2, 5, 6	1, 2, 4, 5, 6, 7, 8	All	All	All	All	1, 2, 3, 4, 5, 6, 7, 8	1, 2, 3, 5, 6
Lake Trout Char		2	2	2, 3, 8	2, 3, 5, 6, 7, 8	2, 3, 5, 6, 7, 8	2, 3, 5, 6, 7, 8	2, 3, 5, 6, 7, 8	2, 3, 5, 6, 7, 8	2, 3, 5, 6, 7, 8	2, 3, 8	

Species	Jan.	Feb.	Mar.	Apr.	May	June	July	Aug.	Sept.	Oct.	Nov.	Dec.
Kokanee Salmon	2, 4, 8	2, 3, 4	1, 2, 4, 8	1, 2, 3, 4, 5, 6, 8	All	All	All	All	All	All		
Rocky Mountain		2, 3, 4	2, 3, 4	2, 3, 4	2, 3, 4	2, 3, 4	2, 3, 4	2, 3, 4	2, 3, 4	2, 3, 4	2, 3, 4	2, 3, 4
Whitefish		5, 6, 8	5, 6, 8	5, 6, 8	5, 6, 7, 8	5, 6, 7, 8	5, 6, 7, 8	5, 6, 7, 8	5, 6, 7, 8	5, 6, 7, 8	5, 8	5, 8
Arctic Grayling					6, 7	6, 7	6, 7	6, 7	6, 7	6, 7		
Pike					6, 7	6, 7	6, 7	6, 7	6, 7	6, 7		
Largemouth Bass			4, 8	4, 8	4, 8	4, 8	4, 8	4, 8	4, 8	4, 8	4, 8	
Smallmouth Bass		1	1, 4, 8	1, 4, 8	1, 4, 8	1, 4, 8	1, 4, 8	1, 4, 8	1, 4, 8	1, 4, 8	1, 4, 8	
Coho Salmon				1, 2	1, 2, 6	1, 2, 5, 6	1, 2, 5, 6	1, 2, 5, 6	1, 2, 5, 6	1, 2, 5, 6	1, 2	2
Chinook Salmon						5, 6	1, 2, 3, / 5, 6	1, 2, 3, / 5, 6	1, 2			
Pink Salmon							1, 2, 5, 6	1, 2, 5, 6				
Sockeye Salmon							2, 6	2, 6	2			
Chum Salmon								5, 6	1, 2, 5, 6	1, 2	1, 2	1, 2

Legend:

All = All Regions
1 = Vancouver Island
2 = Lower Mainland
3 = Thompson–Nicola
4 = Kootenay
5 = Cariboo
6 = Skeena
7 = Omineca–Peace
8 = Okanagan

Note: Regulations may vary from water to water even though species available.

Appendix B: Licenses and Regulations

THE PROVINCIAL FISHERIES BRANCH regulates non-tidal angling in British Columbia with the exception of those waters located in National Parks. If you plan to fish waters located in Kootenay or Yoho or other National Parks, you will need a license issued by Parks Canada. For the remainder of the province, anyone 16 years of age or older must have a basic license to sport fish.

Annual, 1-day and 8-day basic licenses are issued with a reduced rate for British Columbia residents who are disabled or 65 years and older. Licenses can be purchased at most sporting goods stores, fishing resorts or government agent offices.

Besides having an angling quota and requiring that fish kept must be recorded on the license, angling for some species of sport fish such as steelhead, salmon, Kootenay Lake rainbow, Shuswap Lake rainbow and Shuswap Lake char attract additional conservation surcharges. You must purchase a conservation surcharge stamp to fish for steelhead, but on Kootenay and Shuswap lakes you require the surcharge stamp if you intend to keep rainbows 20 in (50 cm) or greater or char 24 in (60 cm) or greater in length. You must purchase a salmon conservation stamp if you wish to fish and keep any legal-sized salmon from non-tidal water. There is an adult chinook annual quota, but only adults need to be recorded. An adult chinook is defined as a chinook 20 in (50 cm) or greater in most regions. However, some waters in Regions 2, 5 and 6 have a larger size designation for an adult chinook. Ensure that you check the regulations for waters you intend to fish for chinooks in Regions 2, 5 and 6. Chinooks less that the legal adult size may be kept and do not need to be recorded on the angling license.

All classified waters attract additional fees. British Columbia residents pay an annual fee that is good for all classified waters, while Canadian residents and non-Canadians are charged daily fees.

For all licenses—basic, conservation surcharge and classified waters—there are three fee structures with a preference given to British Columbia residents. The basic license charges differ for Canadians and non-Canadians, but both those groups pay the same amount for conservation surcharge stamps and to fish classified waters.

The Federal Department of Fisheries and Oceans governs tidal angling. All anglers 16 years and older must purchase a tidal waters license and, to fish for salmon, a salmon conservation stamp. Tidal licenses are available as annual, 1-day, 3-day or 5-day with accompanying escalating fee structure. There is a reduced-fee license for Canadian residents 65 years of age and older.

Both tidal and non-tidal annual basic licenses are in effect from April 1 or later purchase date to March 31 of the following year. Angling licenses must be carried on your person when fishing. On classified waters for those paying a daily fee, the name of the stream and date must be written on the license before angling each day. British Columbia has one limited-entry fishery and that is the Dean River. Non-residents of Canada wanting to fish the Dean are permitted only one 8-day maximum license per year and must enter a draw to get a spot.

There are a few freshwater non-tidal definitions that are of particular interest to fly fishers and at first glance may cause confusion:

An *artificial fly* is defined as a single hook covered with various materials such as fur, feathers, textiles, tinsel or wire.

Artificial Flies gear restriction means that in waters so designated the only type of lure allowed is an artificial fly. Anglers may attach to their line a float and/or an unpainted sinker, but no flasher or spinner. Under this regulation, a spin fisher can use a bubble float and artificial fly. It permits fly fishers to use a flotation device such as a strike indicator or to attach a split shot to the line. On fly-fishing-only-designated waters you cannot use external sinkers or floats on the line. That means that you cannot attach a split shot or strike indicator to the line. However, you may dress your flies with a lead or wire underbody or grease the leader with floatant and colour the line so that it is more noticeable.

Appendix C: Contacts

Fisheries Branch: Each region has personnel whose main job is to manage the fishery for present and future generations of anglers to enjoy. Regional staff can be contacted to get information or clarification about Freshwater Fishing Regulations. However, they do not provide information on where to go fishing. They do manage freshwater guide licenses and can tell you what guides are licensed for particular waters. They cannot, however, recommend individual guides. You have to take the advice given in Chapter 3 and do your own hiring or book through a reputable lodge.

Office addresses and phone numbers for the regions are published on page 1 of the *Freshwater Fishing Regulations Synopsis*, which is available at all fishing shops or government agents' offices.

BC Parks: There are 11 districts managing the provincial parks and many of the districts produce tourist booklets on their parks. Also available and covering the whole province are two government publications on parks: Publication No. 29: *Provincial Parks in British Columbia* and *Parks Guide and Road Map*. Publication 29 is available through writing BC Parks, 2nd floor - 800 Johnson St., Victoria, BC, V8V 1X4 or through the Internet (http://www.env.gov.bc.ca). The *Parks Guide and Road Map* is sold through Davenport Maps, 201 - 2160 Douglas St., Victoria, BC, V8T 4M1, phone (250) 384-2621.

Tourism British Columbia: They produce a wide variety of tourist-related publications, including freshwater and saltwater destination places, which are available through writing Tourism BC, Box 9830, Stn Prov. Govt. TG, Victoria, BC, V8W 9W5 or call toll free in North America 1-800-663-6000, (604) 663-6000 in Greater Vancouver or (250) 387-1642 from overseas.

Forest Service: The province is divided into 6 forest regions with each then broken down into districts. All districts produce maps showing their road system and recreational sites. The maps can be obtained from the Forest Service regional or district offices.

To get information for Fisheries Branch Regional, Parks Districts, Tourism Regional and Forest Service Regional and District offices through the regular 8-to-5, Monday-to-Friday work week call Enquiry BC at 1-800-663-7867 or if in Greater Vancouver (604) 660-2421. Enquiry BC may be able to patch you through toll-free to regional offices so that you can obtain the information specific to your destination.

Many government departments have web pages on the Internet. For British Columbia vacation and adventure opportunities visit:

http://travel.bc.ca

http://bcadventure.com/adventure/index.html

and for information on fisheries and parks visit:

http://www.env.gov.bc.ca

FISHING ADVENTURES

Many freshwater fishing resort owners belong to the British Columbia Fishing Resort and Outfitters Association. Each year the association produces a booklet highlighting many of the province's fishing opportunities and listing their members. A copy of the booklet can be obtained by contacting the association at Box 3301, Kamloops, BC, V2C 6B9, phone: (250) 374-6836 or Fax: (250) 374-6640 or visit their web site at: http://www.oppub.com/bcfroa/bcfroa.html

For tidal fishing contact Tourism BC. However, with a few exceptions saltwater lodge owners sell big dead fish and lots of them and are years behind their freshwater counterparts in recognizing the potential for fly fishing.

Appendix D: References

STILLWATER FLY FISHING BOOKS

Steve Raymond, *Kamloops* (Portland, OR: Frank Amato Publications, 1994, 3rd ed.), ISBN: 1-878175-73-4. The first edition of Steve Raymond's *Kamloops* was released in 1971 and is now a sought-after collector's item. The latest edition has been revised, updated and reformatted into a full-colour production. This is a must book for those fly fishers interested in British Columbia's stillwater fisheries. Raymond includes sections on history of the fishery and fish, managing the resource, trout food, fly patterns, tackle and techniques and closes with a discussion of some of his favourite waters.

Karl Bruhn, *Best of B. C. Lake Fishing* (Vancouver, BC: Whitecap Books, 1992), ISBN: 1-878175-2809. Karl Bruhn, an outdoor writer for many years and former editor of British Columbia's largest outdoor publication, *BC Outdoors*, spent a decade wandering the regions of the province sampling lakes. From the mound of information collected he compiled a selection of 550 of the more promising fishing lakes. For the lake fly fisher interested in learning more on local or distant waters this is a good companion book to other where-to publications.

Brian Chan, *Flyfishing Strategies for Stillwaters* (Kamloops, BC: self published, 1991), ISBN: 0-9695533-0-7. Brian Chan is one of the most well-known of British Columbia's stillwater fly fishers. A biologist working for the provincial Fisheries Branch in Kamloops for most of the past 25 years, Chan combined his knowledge and experience gained from working as professional biologist and as a long-time flyfisher to produce this pocket guide for stillwater fly fishers. The book provides information on the seasons and anatomy of an Interior trout lake, entomology and insect availability, fishing strategies and pattern selection.

RIVER FLY FISHING BOOKS

Rob Brown, *Skeena Steelhead River Journal* (Portland, OR: Frank Amato Publications, 1996), ISBN: 1-57188-32-1. Rob Brown lives in Terrace, where local anglers are treated to his weekly column, "The Skeena Angler," in the *Terrace Standard*. Brown is the consummate storyteller and in this book there are a number of anecdotes about the waters near and dear to his heart on the Lower Skeena. He includes a section on flies for Skeena steelhead, trout and salmon, many uniquely named, and all shown on a full two-page colour plate. Complementing the text are many colour photographs, making this book not only a pleasant read but for the visitor to the area a sumptuous pictorial reminder of the Lower Skeena, its tributaries, its fish and its wildlife.

Arthur J. Lingren, *River Journal: Thompson River* (Portland, OR: Frank Amato Publications, 1994), ISBN: 1-878175-47-5. The Thompson is home to some of the finest, biggest and hardest-fighting summer-run steelhead in the world. After enjoying this fishery for a quarter of a century, I decided that I should put pen to paper and share my knowledge and experiences on this magnificent river. The result was a book that recorded the history of the sport and the history of the steelhead, with a section on fly fishing techniques and flies and details on the best steelhead fishing runs in the Thompson system. I have been criticized by my peers for providing too much information, but I felt I needed to make a record of what was happening at this point in time on this great fishery.

SALTWATER FLY FISHING BOOKS

Jim Crawford, *Salmon to a Fly: Fly Fishing For Salmon in the Open Ocean* (Portland, OR: Frank Amato Publications, 1995), ISBN: 1-57188-034-8. For those fly fishers interested in more information of open-ocean fly fishing for Pacific salmon this book is a must. Jim Crawford provides plenty of information on tackle and salmon but devotes most of the book to places to go on the Queen Charlotte Islands, northern Vancouver Island, mid-Island around Campbell River and the hot spots on the outer coast: Kyuquot, Nootka Island, Clayoquot and Barkley sounds. However, as a river fisher foremost, I, as will many other anglers who enjoy that pastime, differ with Crawford on his objection to fishing for salmon in fresh water.

Steve Raymond, *The Estuary Flyfisher* (Portland, OR: Frank Amato Publications, 1996), ISBN: 1-57188-060-7. Steve Raymond, in this all-colour book, discusses many topics—from the natures of estuaries, tides, salmon and other game fish, to tackle and fly patterns—that fly fishers need to consider when fishing estuaries. Although not specific to British Columbia, the tactics used to fish estuaries and the fish mentioned apply to British Columbia. For the beach fly fisher this is a worthwhile addition to the library.

Barry Thornton, *Saltwater Fly Fishing* (Surrey, BC: Hancock House, 1995), ISBN: 0-88839-319-9. Living in Courtenay, Barry Thornton based this collection of yarns about the salmon, open-ocean and estuary fly fishing, tackle, equipment and flies from experience garnered from fishing the waters in the upper part of the Strait of Georgia over a period of many years. Thornton's book is more useful to Vancouver Island's upper east coast fly fishers. For those wanting to fish other waters, I recommend Crawford's *Salmon to a Fly: Fly Fishing For Salmon in the Open Ocean.*

GENERAL FLY FISHING BOOKS

The Gilly (Kelowna, BC: British Columbia Federation of Fly Fishers, 9th printing 1997), ISBN: 0-88925-638-1. Ever since editor Alf Davy in conjunction with the B.C. Federation of Flyfishers published this guide to British Columbia flyfishing in 1985, the book has received widespread acclaim and has been on the Canadian bestseller's list. Contributing authors, including the editor, cover many subjects from basic equipment and casting techniques, insects and fishes with chapters devoted to fly fishing for summer and winter steelhead, sea-run cutthroat and saltwater salmon fly fishing with a selection of flies for B.C. waters. This is an excellent general book with much useful information and a precursor to more detailed books.

Van Egan, *Waterside Reflections* (Portland, OR: Frank Amato Publications, 1996), ISBN: 1-57188-040-2. Van Egan moved to British Columbia from Wisconsin in the 1950s and bought a house a couple of doors upriver from

Roderick Haig-Brown. Egan, with his easy to read style, reflects on his many experiences gained through a lifetime of fishing. Although the early years are devoted to his experiences on U.S. waters, the later years are about British Columbia and he closes the book with a chapter on his friend of many years, Haig-Brown. If you like to read well-written stories about fishing, *Waterside Reflections* is highly recommended.

Arthur J. Lingren, *Fly Patterns of British Columbia* (Portland, OR: Frank Amato Publications, 1996), ISBN: 1-57188-068-2 (pbk) or 1-57188-069-0 (cloth). British Columbia has as rich a fly fishing history as anywhere in North America and in my opinion second only to that of Great Britain. Rightly so because we owe much of our roots to those early British immigrants. My goal in writing this book was to show the development of the sport of fly fishing through the flies that were produced for interior trout, steelhead, coastal trout and saltwater salmon. Many of the patterns are historic, but many are tried and proven patterns in use today.

WE SHOULD BE SUPPORTING businesses in our communities and especially those that cater to specific hobbies such as fly fishing. Please check local fishing and book stores first, but not all fishing stores stock a wide variety of British Columbia fly-fishing books if any at all. However, with ISBN, author's name, book title and publisher, any bookstore can get any title listed here quite easily. Failing those avenues, Michael & Young Fly Shop in Surrey is an excellent source. They try to keep on hand most British Columbia fly-fishing books. Their address is 10484 137th St., Surrey, B.C. V3T 4H5, phone: (604) 588-2833, Fax: (604) 582-9627 or e-mail: sales@myflyshop.com. Frank Amato Publications in Portland, Oregon, deals directly with the public and copies of his books can be ordered by calling toll free 1-800-541-9498 or by sending a fax to: (503) 653-2766 or by sending an e-mail to: fap@teleport.com. If your local fly shop does not have Brian Chan's *Flyfishing Strategies for Stillwaters*, you can order it direct from Chan by writing to Riseform Flyfishing Ventures, 1832 Orchard Drive, Kamloops, B.C. V2C 4H1.

ATLAS, DIRECTORIES, GUIDE BOOKS

BC Outdoors Fishing Directory & Atlas: Freshwater Edition (Vancouver: OP Publishing Ltd.). This guide and atlas is released yearly and includes descriptions of lakes, rivers, types of fish and available accommodations. There are about 50 maps covering the entire province, showing roads, lakes and rivers, campsites and parks with a grid system for easy location. Each year two of the eight regions are updated so that over a four-year period all the information and maps are checked and updated. This publication is a highly recommended complement to this book. *BC Outdoors* also publishes a saltwater edition, which is useful in finding those coho and chinook hot spots.

Backroad and Outdoor Recreation Mapbook or *Backroad Mapbook* (Surrey, BC: Mussio Ventures). Each book in this growing series contains a mountain of information on a variety of outdoor activities from camping to hiking and fishing. The maps are well detailed and are updated with the latest information every two to three years. Volumes I and II, besides covering freshwater fishing spots, include information on saltwater destinations with maps pinpointing the hot spots.

The series to date is: Vol. I: Southwestern B.C., Vol. II: Vancouver Island, Vol. III: Kamloops/Okanagan, Vol. IV: The Kootenays, Vol. V: The Cariboo and Vol. VI: Prince George to Smithers.

If you are planning a vacation into a specific region, and especially if you want to pursue more than one outdoor activity, these books are an excellent resource and a complement to this book. However, the volumes are not aligned with the Fisheries Branch Management Regions. If you were going to fish Region 3, for example, and move around a fair amount, you would need to have Mussio's Vol. I, Vol. III and Vol. IV.

Cariboo Chilcotin Fishing Guide (Williams Lake, BC: Cariboo Press). This is a locally produced fishing guide detailing those waters with road access in the Cariboo region. Details provided include information on stocking, size and type of fish, location, best times, boat launching and camping or resort accommodation. The accompanying maps are not as detailed as those found in

Mussio Ventures or BC Outdoors directories, but because it is local the information may be more current than in those other publications. The *Cariboo Chilcotin Fishing Guide* is published in the spring of the year and is available in local fishing shops or through the publisher at 188 N. 1st. Avenue, Williams Lake, BC, V2G 1Y8 or calling (250) 392-2331.

PERIODICALS

There are no periodicals devoted strictly to fly fishing in British Columbia. However, all the following magazines do include some fly-fishing information with *BC Outdoors* providing the broadest coverage.

BC Outdoors is the most popular magazine for fishing and hunting enthusiasts in British Columbia. Although general in nature, there are many well-known British Columbia fly-fishing authors contributing to each issue. Included in each issue is an outdoor directory where resorts and guides advertise outdoor adventures. *BC Outdoors* is available at most newsstands and fishing shops or through subscription. Phone: (604) 606-4644 or Fax: (604) 687-1925 or e-mail: oppubl@istar.ca

British Columbia Sport Fishing devotes most of its space to saltwater salmon fishing opportunities, but in each issue there are usually fly-fishing articles, mostly on freshwater. In each issue there is a lodge directory where saltwater lodges predominate. This magazine is available at newsstands or through subscription. Phone: (604) 521-4901.

Island Fish Finder covers saltwater salmon and steelhead on Vancouver Island and coastal British Columbia, with some space devoted to fly fishing and fly tying. Some resort advertising is included in each issue, mostly saltwater, with WeighWest Marine Resort at Tofino the only advertiser catering to the saltwater fly-fishing angler. Available in sport shops and newsstands on Vancouver Island and Sunshine Coast or by subscription. Phone: (250) 954-1200, Fax: (250) 248-8049, e-mail: fishfind@nanaimo.ark.com or on the Internet at www.bc-travel.com/ci/fishfinder.html

HYDROGRAPHIC CHARTS

Saltwater flyfishers who intend to do their own boating need hydrographic charts. Contact the Canadian Hydrographic Service, Dept. of Fisheries and Oceans, P.O. Box 6000, Sidney, BC, V8L 4B2 to receive their catalogue of Pacific Coast nautical charts.

Inside Out British Columbia

A Best Places ® Guide to the Outdoors

Jack Christie

From Pender Harbour to Yoho National Park, from the Queen Charlottes to Kamloops, recreational writer and outdoor columnist Jack Christie's *Inside Out British Columbia* tells where, when and how to enjoy the best outdoor activities in the province—many within an hour of Vancouver. Setting itself apart from all other guidebooks to B.C., *Inside Out British Columbia* covers not only the Lower Mainland and Vancouver Island, but also the Gulf Islands, the central coast, the central and southern interior, the Okanagan, the East and West Kootenays and the northeastern and northwestern extremities of the province. No matter the season or skill level, with this comprehensive and handy guide readers can explore beaches, bike, camp, fish, hike, horseback ride, kayak, river raft, ski, watch wildlife and much more *all over* the province. And for travellers who want to temper rugged adventure with a little comfort, star-rated accommodations and dining options are included.

softbound, 9 maps, 576 pages approx.

$26.95, ISBN 1-55192-131-6

RAINCOAST BOOKS
8680 Cambie Street, Vancouver, B.C. V6P 6M9 1-800-663-5714